Test Yourself

Cognitive Psychology

Test Yourself... Psychology Series

Test Yourself

Cognitive Psychology

Dominic Upton and Penney Upton

Multiple-Choice Questions prepared by Emma L. Preece

LearningMatters

First published in 2011 by Learning Matters Ltd

British Library Cataloguing in Publication Data
A CIP record for this book is available from the British Library

ISBN: 978 0 85725 669 0

This book is also available in the following e-book formats:
Adobe ebook ISBN: 978 0 85725 671 3
EPUB book ISBN: 978 0 85725 670 6
Kindle ISBN: 978 0 85725 672 0

Cover design by Toucan Design
Text design by Toucan Design
Project Management by Deer Park Productions, Tavistock, Devon
Typeset by Pantek Media, Maidstone, Kent
Printed and bound in Great Britain by Bell & Bain Ltd, Glasgow

Learning Matters Ltd
20 Cathedral Yard
Exeter
EX1 1HB
Tel: 01392 215560
info@learningmatters.co.uk
www.learningmatters.co.uk

Contents

Acknowledgements

The production of this series has been a rapid process with an apparent deadline at almost every turn. We are therefore grateful to colleagues both from Learning Matters (Julia Morris and Helen Fairlie) and the University of Worcester for making this process so smooth and (relatively) effortless. In particular we wish to thank our colleagues for providing many of the questions, specifically:

- Biological Psychology: Emma Preece
- Cognitive Psychology: Emma Preece
- Developmental Psychology: Charlotte Taylor
- Personality and Individual Differences: Daniel Kay
- Research Methods and Design in Psychology: Laura Scurlock-Evans
- Social Psychology: Laura Scurlock-Evans

Finally, we must, once again, thank our children (Gabriel, Rosie and Francesca) for not being as demanding as usual during the process of writing and development.

Introduction

Psychology is one of the most exciting subjects that you can study at university in the twenty-first century. A degree in psychology helps you to understand and explain thought, emotion and behaviour. You can then apply this knowledge to a range of issues in everyday life including health and well-being, performance in the workplace, education – in fact any aspect of life you can think of! However, a degree in psychology gives you much more than a set of 'facts' about mind and behaviour; it will also equip you with a wide range of skills and knowledge. Some of these, such as critical thinking and essay writing, have much in common with humanities subjects, while others such as hypothesis testing and numeracy are scientific in nature. This broad-based skill set prepares you exceptionally well for the workplace – whether or not your chosen profession is in psychology. Indeed, recent evidence suggests employers appreciate the skills and knowledge of psychology graduates. A psychology degree really can help you get ahead of the crowd. However, in order to reach this position of excellence, you need to develop your skills and knowledge fully and ensure you complete your degree to your highest ability.

This book is designed to enable you, as a psychology student, to maximise your learning potential by assessing your level of understanding and your confidence and competence in cognitive psychology, one of the core knowledge domains for psychology. It does this by providing you with essential practice in the types of questions you will encounter in your formal university assessments. It will also help you make sense of your results and identify your strengths and weaknesses. This book is one part of a series of books designed to assist you with learning and developing your knowledge of psychology. The series includes books on:

- Biological Psychology
- Cognitive Psychology
- Developmental Psychology
- Personality and Individual Differences
- Research Methods and Design in Psychology
- Social Psychology

In order to support your learning this book includes over 200 targeted Multiple-Choice Questions (MCQs) and Extended Multiple-Choice Questions (EMCQs) that have been carefully put together to help assess your depth of knowledge of cognitive psychology. The MCQs are split into two formats: the foundation level questions are about your level of understanding of the key principles and components of key areas in psychology.

Hopefully, within these questions you should recognise the correct answer from the four options. The advanced level questions require more than simple recognition – some will require recall of key information, some will require application of this information and others will require synthesis of information. At the end of each chapter you will find a set of essay questions covering each of the topics. These are typical of the kinds of question that you are likely to encounter during your studies. In each chapter, the first essay question is broken down for you using a concept map, which is intended to help you develop a detailed answer to the question. Each of the concept maps is shaded to show you how topics link together, and includes cross-references to relevant MCQs in the chapter. You should be able to see a progression in your learning from the foundation to the advanced MCQs, to the extended MCQs and finally the essay questions. The book is divided up into 10 chapters and your cognitive psychology module is likely to have been divided into similar topic areas. However, do not let this restrict your thinking in relation to cognitive psychology: these topics interact. The sample essay questions, which complement the questions provided in the chapter, will help you to make the links between different topic areas. You will find the answers to all of the MCQs and EMCQs at the end of the book. There is a separate table of answers for each chapter; use the self monitoring column in each of the tables to write down your own results, coding correct answers as NC, incorrect answers as NI and any you did not respond to as NR. You can then use the table on page 99 to analyse your results.

The aim of the book is not only to help you revise for your exams, it is also intended to help with your learning. However, it is not intended to replace lectures, seminars and tutorials, or to supersede the book chapters and journal articles signposted by your lecturers. What this book can do, however, is set you off on a sound footing for your revision and preparation for your exams. In order to help you to consolidate your learning, the book also contains tips on how to approach MCQ assessments and how you can use the material in this text to assess, *and enhance*, your knowledge base and level of understanding.

Now you know the reasons behind this book and how it will enhance your success, it is time for you to move on to the questions – let the fun begin!

Assessing your interest, competence and confidence

The aim of this book is to help you to maximise your learning potential by assessing your level of understanding, confidence and competence in core issues in psychology. So how does it do this?

Assessing someone's knowledge of a subject through MCQs might at first glance seem fairly straightforward: typically the MCQ consists of a question, one correct answer and one or more incorrect answers, sometimes called distractors. For example, in this book each question has one right answer and three distractors. The goal of an MCQ test is for you to get every question right and so show just how much knowledge you have. However, because you are given a number of answers to select from, you might be able to choose the right answer either by guessing or by a simple process of elimination – in other words by knowing what is not the right answer. For this reason it is sometimes argued that MCQs only test knowledge of facts rather than in-depth understanding of a subject. However, there is increasing evidence that MCQs can also be valuable at a much higher level of learning, if used in the right way (see, for example, Gardner-Medwin and Gahan, 2003). They can help you to develop as a self-reflective learner who is able to recognise the interest you have in a subject matter as well as your level of competence and confidence in your own knowledge.

MCQs can help you gauge your interest, competence and confidence in the following way. It has been suggested (Howell, 1982) that there are four possible states of knowledge (see Table 1). Firstly, it is possible that you do not know something and are not aware of this lack of knowledge. This describes the naive learner – think back to your first week at university when you were a 'fresher' student and had not yet begun your psychology course. Even if you had done psychology at A level, you were probably feeling a little self-conscious and uncertain in this new learning environment. During the first encounter in a new learning situation most of us feel tentative and unsure of ourselves; this is because we don't yet know what it is we don't know – although to feel this lack of certainty suggests that we know there is something we don't know, even if we don't yet know what this is! In contrast, some people appear to be confident and at ease even in new learning situations; this is not usually because they already know everything but rather because they too do not yet know what it is they do not know – but they have yet to even acknowledge that there is a gap in their knowledge. The next step on from this 'unconscious non-competence' is 'conscious non-competence'; once you started your psychology course you began to realise what the gaps were in your knowledge – you now knew what you didn't know! While this can be an uncomfortable feeling, it is important for the learning process that this acknowledgement of a gap in knowledge is made, because it is the first step in reaching the next level of learning – that of a 'conscious competent' learner. In other words you need to know what the gap in your knowledge is so that you can fill it.

Table 1 Consciousness and competence in learning

	Unconscious	**Conscious**
Non-competent	You don't know something and are not aware that you lack this knowledge/skill.	You don't know something and are aware that you lack this knowledge/skill.
Competent	You know something but are not aware of your knowledge/skill.	You know something and are aware of your knowledge/skill.

One of the ways this book can help you move from unconscious non-competency to conscious competency should by now be clear – it can help you identify the gaps in your knowledge. However, if used properly it can do much more; it can also help you to assess your consciousness and competence in this knowledge.

When you answer an MCQ, you will no doubt have a feeling about how confident you are about your answer: 'I know the answer to question 1 is A. Question 2 I am not so sure about. I am certain the answer is not C or D, so it must be A or B. Question 3, I haven't got a clue so I will say D – but that is a complete guess.' Sound familiar? Some questions you know the answers to, you have that knowledge and know you have it; other questions you are less confident about but think you may know which (if not all) are the distractors, while for others you know this is something you just don't know. Making use of this feeling of confidence will help you become a more reflective – and therefore effective – learner.

Perhaps by now you are wondering where we are going with this and how any of this can help you learn. 'Surely all that matters is whether or not I get the answers right? Does that show I have knowledge?' Indeed it may well do and certainly, if you are confident in your answers, then yes it does. But what if you were not sure? What if your guess of D for our fictional question 3 above was correct? What if you were able to complete all the MCQs in a test and score enough to pass – but every single answer was a guess? Do you really know and understand psychology because you have performed well – and will you be able to do the same again if you retake the test next week? Take a look back at Table 1. If you are relying on guesswork and hit upon the answer by accident you might perform well without actually understanding how you know the answer, or that you even knew it (unconscious competence), or you may not realise you don't know something (unconscious non-competence). According to this approach to using

MCQs what is important is not how many answers you get right, but whether or not you acknowledge your confidence in the answer you give: it is better to get a wrong answer and acknowledge it is wrong (so as to work on filling that gap).

Therefore what we recommend you do when completing the MCQs is this: for each answer you give, think about how confident you are that it is right. You might want to rate each of your answers on the following scale:

3:    I am confident this is the right answer.

2:    I am not sure, but I think this is the right answer.

1:    I am not sure, but I think this is the wrong answer.

0:    I am confident this is the wrong answer.

Using this system of rating your confidence will help you learn for yourself both what you know and what you don't know. You will become a conscious learner through the self-directed activities contained in this book. Reflection reinforces the links between different areas of your learning and knowledge and strengthens your ability to *justify* an answer, so enabling you to perform to the best of your ability.

References

Gardner-Medwin, A.R. and Gahan, M. (2003) *Formative and Summative Confidence-Based Assessment*, Proceedings of 7th International Computer-Aided Assessment Conference, Loughborough, UK, July, pp. 147–55.

Howell, W.C. (1982) 'An overview of models, methods, and problems', in W.C. Howell and E.A. Fleishman (eds), *Human Performance and Productivity, Vol. 2: Information Processing and Decision Making*. Hillsdale, NJ: Erlbaum.

Tips for success: how to succeed in your assessments

This book, part of a comprehensive new series, will help you achieve your psychology aspirations. It is designed to assess your knowledge so that you can review your current level of performance and where you need to spend more time and effort reviewing and revising material. However, it hopes to do more than this – it aims to assist you with your learning so it not only acts as an assessor of performance but as an aid to learning. Obviously, it is not a replacement for every single text, journal article, presentation and abstract you will read and review during the course of your degree programme. Similarly, it is in no way a replacement for your lectures, seminars or additional reading – it should complement all of this material. However, it will also add something to all of this other material: learning is assisted by reviewing and assessing and this is what this text aims to do – help you learn through assessing your learning.

The focus throughout this book, as it is in all of the books in this series, is on how you should approach and consider your topics in relation to assessment and exams. Various features have been included to help you build up your skills and knowledge ready for your assessments.

This book, and the other companion volumes in this series, should help you learn through testing and assessing yourself – it should provide an indication of how advanced your thinking and understanding is. Once you have assessed your understanding you can explore what you need to learn and how. However, hopefully, quite a bit of what you read here you will already have come across and the text will act as a reminder and set your mind at rest – you do know your material.

Succeeding at MCQs

Exams based on MCQs are becoming more and more frequently used in higher education and particularly in psychology. As such you need to know the best strategy for completing such assessments and succeeding. The first thing to note is, if you know the material then the questions will present no problems – so revise and understand your notes and back this up with in-depth review of material presented in textbooks, specialist materials and journal articles. However, once you have done this you need to look at the technique for answering multiple-choice questions and here are some tips for success:

1. Time yourself. The first important thing to note when you are sitting your examination is the time available to you for completing it. If you have, for example, an hour and a half to answer 100 multiple-choice questions this means you have 54 seconds to complete each question. This means that you have to read, interpret, think about and select one answer for a multiple-choice question in under a minute. This may seem impossible, but there are several things that you can do to use your time effectively.

2. Practise. By using the examples in this book, those given out in your courses, in class tests or on the web you can become familiar with the format and wording of multiple-choice questions similar to those used in your exam. Another way of improving your chances is to set your own multiple-choice exams – try and think of some key questions and your four optional responses (including the correct one of course!). Try and think of optional distractors that are sensible and not completely obvious. You could, of course, swap questions with your peers – getting them to set some questions for you while you set some questions for them. Not only will this help you with your practice but you will also understand the format of MCQs and the principles underlying their construction – this will help you answer the questions when it comes to the real thing.

3. The rule of totality. Look out for words like 'never' and 'always' in multiple-choice questions. It is rare in psychology for any answer to be true in relation to these words of 'totality'. As we all know, psychology is a multi-modal subject that has multiple perspectives and conflicting views and so it is very unlikely that there will always be a 'never' or an 'always'. When you see these words, focus on them and consider them carefully. A caveat is, of course, sometimes never and always will appear in a question, but be careful of these words!

4. Multiple, multiple-choice answers. Some multiple-choice answers will contain statements such as 'both A and C' or 'all of the above' or 'none of these'. Do not be distracted by these choices. Multiple-choice questions have only one correct answer and do not ask for opinion or personal bias. Quickly go through each choice independently, crossing off the answers that you know are not true. If, after eliminating the incorrect responses, you think there is more than one correct answer, group your answers and see if one of the choices matches yours. If you believe only one answer is correct, do not be distracted by multiple-choice possibilities.

5. 'First guess is best' fallacy. There is a myth among those who take (or even write) MCQs that the 'first guess is best'. This piece of folklore is misleading: research (and psychologists love research) indicates that when people change their answers on an MCQ exam, about two-thirds of the time they go from wrong to right, showing that the first guess is often not the best. So, think about it and consider your answer – is it right? Remember, your first guess is not better than a result obtained through good, hard, step-by-step, conscious thinking that enables you to select the answer that you believe to be the best.

6. The rule of threes. One of the most helpful strategies for multiple-choice questions is a three-step process:

(i)   Read the question thoroughly but quickly. Concentrate on particular words such as 'due to' and 'because' or 'as a result of' and on words of totality such as 'never' or 'always' (although see rule 3 above).

(ii) Rather than going to the first answer you think is correct (see rule 5) eliminate the ones that you think are wrong one by one. While this may take more time, it is more likely to provide the correct answer. Furthermore, answer elimination may provide a clue to a misread answer you may have overlooked.

(iii) Reread the question, as if you were reading it for the first time. Now choose your answer from your remaining answers based on this rereading.

7. Examine carefully. Examine each of the questions carefully, particularly those that are very similar. It may be that exploring parts of the question will be useful – circle the parts that are different. It is possible that each of the alternatives will be very familiar and hence you must **understand the meaning** of each of the alternatives with respect to the context of the question. You can achieve this by studying for the test as though it will be a short-answer or essay test. Look for the level of **qualifying words**. Such words as *best, always, all, no, never, none, entirely, completely* suggest that a condition exists without exception. Items containing words that provide for some level of exception or qualification are: *often, usually, less, seldom, few, more* and *most* (and see rule 3). If you know that two or three of the options are correct, **'all of the above'** is a strong possibility.

8. Educated guesses. Never leave a question unanswered. If nothing looks familiar, pick the answer that seems most complete and contains the most information. Most of the time (if not all of the time!) the best way to answer a question is to know the answer! However, there may be times when you will not know the answer or will not really understand the question. There are three circumstances in which you should guess: when you are stuck, when you are running out of time, or both of these! Guessing strategies are always dependent on the scoring system used to mark the exam (see the section on MCQ scoring mechanisms). If the multiple-choice scoring system makes the odds of gaining points equal to the odds of having points deducted it does not pay to guess if you are unable to eliminate any of the answers. But the odds of improving your test score are in your favour if you can rule out even one of the answers. The odds in your favour increase as you rule out more answers in any one question. So, take account of the scoring mechanisms and then eliminate, move onwards and guess!

9. Revise and learn. Study carefully and learn your material. The best tip for success is always to learn the material. Use this book, use your material, use your time wisely but, most of all, use your brain!

Chapter 1
Introduction to cognitive psychology

This chapter provides questions relating to the philosophical bases of contemporary cognitive psychology. It includes topics such as schools of thought, the scope of the subject, key terms and concepts, methodological considerations and prominent milestones in research. It will test both your foundation and advanced knowledge of these topics. At the end of the chapter are several example essay questions and a sample concept map which may enable you to organise your thoughts during essay planning.

Select one answer for each question.

Foundation level questions

1. Which of these lists contains a topic that would not be studied in contemporary cognitive psychology?

   A. Language acquisition, reasoning, problem-solving and anxiety.

   B. Dementia, brain damage, depression and semantic memory.

   C. Perception, attention, eyewitness testimony and learning.

   D. None of the above.

   Your answer: ☐

2. Which of these disciplines has not actively contributed towards contemporary cognitive psychology?

   A. Biology.

   B. Sociology.

   C. Computer science.

   D. Philosophy.

   Your answer: ☐

3. Which of the following developments coincided with the onset of the cognitive revolution?

   A. Rise of behaviourism.

   B. Initiation of connectionist modelling.

   C. Invention of the digital computer.

   D. Invention of neuroimaging techniques.

Your answer: ☐

4. Which of these lists contains an experimental technique not used in cognitive psychology?

   A. Observation, psychodrama and neuroimaging.

   B. Laboratory experiments, case studies and computer simulations.

   C. Neuroimaging, case studies and observation.

   D. Questionnaires, laboratory experiments and case studies.

Your answer: ☐

5. Which of these measures cannot be obtained using the methodologies adopted by cognitive psychology?

   A. Eye movement, fixations and saccades.

   B. Reaction times and error rates.

   C. Levels of cortical activation.

   D. None of the above.

Your answer: ☐

6. Naturalistic observation could be used in cognitive psychology for what purpose?

   A. Testing hypotheses.

   B. Identifying cause and effect.

   C. Generating theories and hypotheses.

   D. Identifying relationships between variables.

Your answer: ☐

7. Which branch of cognitive psychology combines experimental techniques, psychobiology, artificial intelligence, connectionist modelling, psycholinguistics, philosophy and anthropology?

   A. Cognitive science.

   B. Neuropsychology.

   C. Neuroscience.

   D. Cognitive-behaviourism.

Your answer: ☐

8. Which of the statements below reflects the term 'ecological validity'?

   A. Whether an experiment is tightly controlled.

   B. Whether an experimental task measures processes which occur in the real world.

   C. Whether an experiment is replicable in other circumstances.

   D. Whether an experiment measures what it claims to.

Your answer: ☐

9. In which branch of cognitive psychology would a double dissociation be interpreted as evidence for a specialised anatomical structure based on case studies of patients with brain damage?

   A. Cognitive neuropsychology.

   B. Cognitive science.

   C. Experimental cognitive psychology.

   D. Cognitive neuroscience.

Your answer: ☐

10. Which of the following theories is not a symbolic model?

   A. Atkinson and Shiffrin's (1971) modal model of memory.

   B. Baddeley and Hitch's (1974) model of working memory.

   C. Caramazza's (1991) dual route model of spelling.

   D. McClelland and Rumelhart's (1981) model of word recognition.

Your answer: ☐

11. Donders (1868) conducted an experiment investigating mental chronometry and obtained what measure?

    A. Cortical activity.

    B. Event-related potentials.

    C. Reaction times.

    D. Verbal protocols.

Your answer: ☐

Advanced level questions

12. Which theory was proposed by Helmholtz (1871)?

    A. Unconscious inference.

    B. Structuralism.

    C. Functionalism.

    D. Social constructionism.

Your answer: ☐

13. Which of these tools would be used in cognitive neuroscience?

    A. Introspection.

    B. Magnetic resonance imaging.

    C. Cognitive interviews.

    D. Role play.

Your answer: ☐

14. Back propagation is a rule used by which form of model?

    A. Semantic.

    B. Connectionist.

    C. Neuropsychological.

    D. Neurological.

Your answer: ☐

15. Which psychologist believed that language acquisition and usage could be explained solely according to environmental contingencies?

A. Lashley (1956).

B. James (1980).

C. Skinner (1957).

D. O'Keefe (1985).

Your answer: ☐

16. Which of the following is not one of Kuhn's (1962) scientific paradigm shifts?

A. Pre-paradigm.

B. Normal science.

C. Revolutionary science.

D. Post-paradigm.

Your answer: ☐

17. Which of these terms is not used by cognitive scientists to mean consciousness according to Kellogg (2003)?

A. Self-concept.

B. Self-knowledge.

C. Informational access.

D. Sentience.

Your answer: ☐

18. Which theoretical antecedent of cognitive psychology lends itself to systematic experimentation investigating cognitive processes?

A. Rationalism.

B. Phenomenology.

C. Empiricism.

D. Idealism.

Your answer: ☐

19. Which school of thought was based on the assumption that experience is determined by a combination of sensations?

A. Phenomenology.

B. Behaviourism.

C. Functionalism.

D. Structuralism.

Your answer: ☐

20. Which tool would be used to analyse perception based on geometric forms, size relations and constituent colours?

A. Connectionism.

B. Introspection.

C. Experimentation.

D. Associationism.

Your answer: ☐

21. Verbal protocols are derived from which task?

A. Thinking aloud.

B. Diary records.

C. Reaction times.

D. Instructing participants.

Your answer: ☐

22. Which method is used by cognitive psychologists to isolate a single stage of processing?

A. Method of subtraction.

B. Method of addition.

C. Method of division.

D. Method of multiplication.

Your answer: ☐

23. Fodor (1973) advocated which approach to mind?

  A. Associationism.

  B. Artificial intelligence.

  C. Phenomenology.

  D. Modularity.

Your answer: ☐

24. According to the mind–body problem, which three terms reflect dualist perspectives?

  A. Idealism, materialism and neutral monism.

  B. Idealism, interactionism and materialism.

  C. Parallelism, interactionism and epiphenomenalism.

  D. Neutral monism, epiphenomenalism and parallelism.

Your answer: ☐

Extended multiple-choice question

Complete the following paragraph using the items listed overleaf. Not all of the items will be consistent with the paragraph and not all items can be used. Items can be used only once.

Laboratory-based experiments in cognitive psychology present the opportunity to manipulate a series of _____ and identify how they impact upon the _____ within a controlled environment. These experiments possess significant validity and _____ when performed correctly. However, multiple-methods often expand the understanding of phenomena. For example, _____ can be combined with traditional experimentation to assess the physiological responses and corresponding cortical activity. _____ in neuropsychology can be combined with traditional experimentation to assess how normal functions may be impaired following brain damage or infection. With regard to connectionism, this technique can be utilised to assess the micro-processes of cognition using computer simulations.

Optional items

A. case studies

B. computer

C. controlled

D. dependent variables

E. developmental

F. independent variables

G. neuroimaging

H. neuropsychology

I. reliability

J. replicable

Essay questions for Chapter 1

Once you have completed the MCQs you are ready to tackle the example essay questions below. You might like to select three or four topics and make notes on them. One way of doing this is to create a concept map. The first question has been done for you and you can see how the knowledge required links to some of the MCQs in this chapter.

1. Critically discuss the claim that contemporary cognitive psychology has more in common with philosophy than science.

2. Critically evaluate the extent to which cognitive psychology can be classed as a science with reference to Kuhn's (1962) theory of scientific revolutions and paradigm shifts.

3. Compare and contrast the origins of two branches of cognitive psychology with reference to their perspectives on the mind–body problem, ideology, methodology, data and research outputs.

4. Evaluate the extent to which dualist perspectives still permeate contemporary cognitive psychology with specific reference to neuropsychology and cognitive science.

5. Critically discuss the claim that no single individual could be said to be the founding father of cognitive psychology.

6. Evaluate the impact of the information processing metaphor within contemporary psychology with reference to two broad topics (e.g. memory and language).

7. Critically discuss the influences of monist and dualist perspectives in contemporary cognitive psychology with reference to both theories and methodology.

8. Critically evaluate the extent to which the cognitive revolution has contributed towards theoretical and methodological advancement with reference to a minimum of two branches of cognitive psychology (e.g. neuroscience and psycholinguistics).

Chapter 1 essay question 1: concept map

Critically discuss the claim that contemporary cognitive psychology has more in common with philosophy than science.

The following concept map presents an example of how your responses to this question could be structured in a meaningful and comprehensive way. There are also links to specific questions in this chapter to guide your revision process. The main influences of science and philosophy are conceptualised through their association with aspects of contemporary cognitive psychology. For example, science has provided tools such as hardware, instruments and software while philosophy guides interpretation of phenomena through its association with each school of thought.

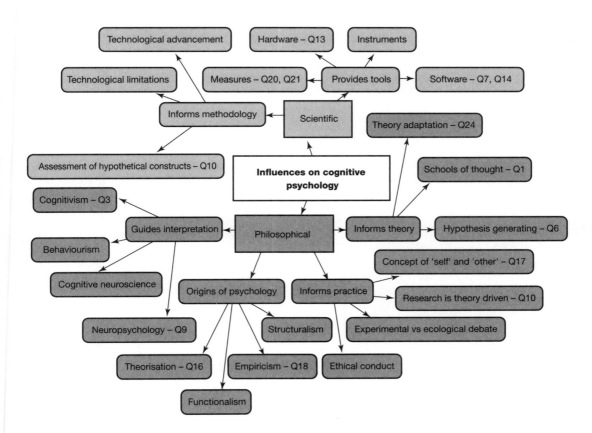

Chapter 2
Perception

This chapter provides questions relating to types of perception (e.g. space, pattern, facial), models of perception (e.g. signal detection, template theory, prototype theories, constructive perception), methodological considerations and research findings (including normal and impaired processing). It will test both your foundation and advanced knowledge of these topics. At the end of the chapter are several example essay questions and a sample concept map which may enable you to organise your thoughts during essay planning.

Select one answer for each question.

Foundation level questions

1. Complete the following sentence according to Gestalt principles: 'The _____ is more important than the sum of its _____.'

   A. parts, whole.

   B. whole, parts.

   C. information, processing.

   D. model, connections.

   Your answer: ☐

2. Which of these terms is not a Gestalt principle?

   A. Semanticity.

   B. Proximity.

   C. Continuity.

   D. Symmetry.

   Your answer: ☐

3. Palmer (1975) demonstrated that which factor can influence perception?

   A. Emotion.

   B. Templates.

   C. Schema.

   D. Context.

Your answer: ☐

4. Simons and Chabris (1999) demonstrated that perception is dependent on which other process?

   A. Attention.

   B. Memory.

   C. Language.

   D. Reason.

Your answer: ☐

5. Who introduced the concepts of distal objects, informational medium, proximal stimulation and perceptual objects?

   A. Durgin (2000).

   B. Hebb (1949).

   C. Gibson (1966).

   D. Tulving (1962).

Your answer: ☐

6. Which of the following is not an aspect of the interactive activation model?

   A. Word level.

   B. Syntax level.

   C. Letter level.

   D. Feature level.

Your answer: ☐

7. Selfridge and Neisser (1960) proposed which type of theory concerning pattern recognition?

   A. Prototype theory.

   B. Template theory.

   C. Feature theory.

   D. Structural theory.

Your answer: ☐

8. According to Lander and Metcalfe (2007), which facial expression is rated as more familiar?

   A. Negative.

   B. Threatening.

   C. Positive.

   D. Anxious.

Your answer: ☐

9. There is an expectation that one word will follow the previous word to aid the preception of language. What is the technical term for this tool?

   A. Transitional probabilities.

   B. Syntax.

   C. Semantics.

   D. Perceptual intelligence.

Your answer: ☐

10. Colour processing is impaired in which of the conditions below?

   A. Akinetopsia.

   B. Anomia.

   C. Visual agnosia.

   D. Achromatopsia.

Your answer: ☐

11. Which of the techniques below is a suitable tool for assessing colour perception?

    A. Stereopsis.

    B. Figure-ground segregation.

    C. Microspectrophotometry.

    D. Filehne illusions.

Your answer: ☐

12. Palmer and Rock (1994) proposed which of the following theories?

    A. Uniform connectedness.

    B. Perceptual segregation.

    C. Size consistency.

    D. Motion parallax.

Your answer: ☐

13. Isomorphism refers to which phenomenon?

    A. Reflected images look identical despite different routes to the visual cortex.

    B. Visual organisation is mirrored by corresponding processes in the brain.

    C. Objects are instantly differentiated from each other based on their boundaries.

    D. Despite changes in expression and appearance faces are still recognised as familiar.

Your answer: ☐

Advanced level questions

14. Which term describes the tendency for cells in the primary visual cortex to be in comparable positions to their receptive fields in the human retina?

    A. Retinotopic map.

    B. Cognitive map.

    C. Pre-visual correspondence.

    D. None of the above.

Your answer: ☐

15. Which of the definitions below refers to perceptual constancy?

    A. All humans perceive objects in the same way irrespective of cognition.

    B. The perceptual bias for faces is universal.

    C. Perception of an object remains the same even when the distal object changes.

    D. Objects appear to be motionless even when they are in motion.

Your answer: ☐

16. Which of these terms refers to when each eye transmits disparate images to the brain?

    A. Monocular disparity.

    B. Size disparity.

    C. Convergence disparity.

    D. Binocular disparity.

Your answer: ☐

17. The retinal flow field refers to which of the items below?

    A. Object recognition based on convergence.

    B. Changes in the pattern of light reflected on the retina.

    C. Corresponding activation between the retina and the visual cortex.

    D. None of the above.

Your answer: ☐

18. In the case of interposition, in which case do objects appear to be further away?

    A. When partially obscuring other objects.

    B. When partially obscured by other objects.

    C. When grains are smaller and closer together.

    D. When the eyes are relaxed.

Your answer: ☐

19. Which of the following is not a component of Biederman's (1987) theory of object perception?

    A. Edge extraction.

    B. Parsing of regions of consistency.

    C. Primal sketch.

    D. Detection of non-accidental properties.

Your answer: ☐

20. Marr (1982) utilised which type of construct in regard to object recognition?

    A. Representations.

    B. Schemas.

    C. Templates.

    D. Models.

Your answer: ☐

21. Biederman (1987) proposed that there were 36 types for which of the following?

    A. Geons.

    B. Objects.

    C. Mental maps.

    D. Junctions.

Your answer: ☐

22. What is the primary distinction between heuristics and algorithms?

    A. Heuristics are procedures guaranteed to solve the problem, algorithms use rules of thumb.

    B. Algorithms are used by humans, heuristics are used by computers.

    C. Heuristics use bottom-up processes, algorithms use top-down processes.

    D. Heuristics use rules of thumb, algorithms are procedures guaranteed to solve the problem.

Your answer: ☐

23. Which type of expectation is responsible for the word superiority effect?

   A. Top-down lexically driven expectations.

   B. Top-down conceptually driven expectations.

   C. Bottom-up semantically driven expectations.

   D. Bottom-up procedurally driven expectations.

Your answer: ☐

24. The theory that all we need to perceive items is the information in our sensory receptors is known as what?

   A. Constructive perception.

   B. Active perception.

   C. Direct perception.

   D. Monocular perception.

Your answer: ☐

25. In the case of perception, which of these perspectives could be considered to be a top-down approach?

   A. Constructive perception.

   B. Recognition by components.

   C. Feature detection.

   D. Structural description.

Your answer: ☐

26. What are the deficits observed in the case of patients with optic ataxia?

   A. Impaired ability of the visual system to identify objects.

   B. Impaired ability of the visual system to perceive binocular cues.

   C. Impaired ability of the visual system to detect patterns.

   D. Impaired ability of the visual system to guide movement.

Your answer: ☐

Extended multiple-choice question

Complete the following paragraph using the items listed below. Not all of the items will be consistent with the paragraph and not all items can be used. Items can be used only once.

The Berlin School, from which the _____ emerged, argued that the brain functions in a holistic manner with a tendency to impose organisation on seemingly random configurations. Consequently, they argued that the entirety of the perceived image takes precedence over the individual components. This is in direct comparison to previous perspectives which drew on _____ such as that advocated by Wundt. Gestalt theorists proposed several principles which can be directly applied to perception. For example, _____ states that there is direct correspondence between conscious experience and the activity observed in the brain. Significantly, the principle of _____ also states that items which are organised in close proximity tend to be perceived as belonging together. Such theories are often demonstrated using

_____ .

Optional items

A. Berlin approach

B. contiguity

C. functionalism

D. interviews

E. Gestalt approach

F. organisation

G. optical illusions

H. physiological approach

I. psychophysical isomorphism

J. structuralism

Essay questions for Chapter 2

Once you have completed the MCQs you are ready to tackle the example essay questions below. You might like to select three or four topics and make notes on them. One way of doing this is to create a concept map. The first question has been done for you and you can see how the knowledge required links to some of the MCQs in this chapter.

1. Evaluate two models of face recognition with reference to both normal and impaired perceptual processing.

2. Critically compare top-down and bottom-up theories of perception, including evidence supporting and refuting each of these accounts.

3. Critically evaluate the contributions of case studies and laboratory experiments investigating impaired perceptual processing.

4. With reference to research investigating object recognition, compare and contrast Marr's (1982) representation theory and Biederman's (1987, 1990) recognition by components theory.

5. Evaluate the extent to which human perception can be investigated and understood within controlled laboratory settings.

6. Discuss the influence of attention and memory on human perception with reference to both normal and impaired performance.

7. Critically discuss the extent to which human perception accurately reflects the actual environment with reference to a minimum of two theories and a broad selection of evidence.

8. To what extent is contemporary research investigating perception still guided by Gestalt principles?

Chapter 2 essay question 1: concept map

Evaluate two models of face recognition with reference to both normal and impaired perceptual processing.

The following concept map presents an example of how your responses to this question could be structured in a meaningful and comprehensive way. There are also links to specific questions in this chapter to guide your revision process. The theories presented by Burton and Bruce (1993) and Bruce and Young (1986) are compared and contrasted for their structures, processes and evidence with explicit examples for each of these aspects.

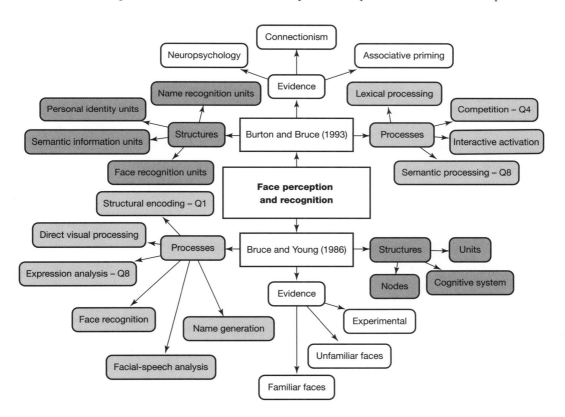

Chapter 3
Attention

This chapter provides questions relating to attention. It includes topics such as schools of thought, the scope of the subject, key terms and concepts, methodological considerations and prominent milestones in attention research. It will test both your foundation and advanced knowledge of these topics. At the end of the chapter are several example essay questions and a sample concept map which may enable you to organise your thoughts during essay planning.

Select one answer for each question.

Foundation level questions

1. The tendency for incongruent printed words to impair colour naming is known as which effect?

    A. Stroop.

    B. Attenuation.

    C. Selective filtering.

    D. Spatial neglect.

    Your answer:

2. Selective attention refers to which of the following?

    A. Attending to numerous stimuli simultaneously.

    B. Attending to a stimulus while ignoring other items.

    C. Ignoring all stimuli through self-control.

    D. Attending to all stimuli through automatic processes.

    Your answer:

3. Marcel (1983) observed which phenomenon?

    A. Automatic filtering of irrelevant information in a crowded room.

    B. Dishabituation after frequent exposure.

    C. Processing of items which were presented too briefly for conscious awareness.

    D. Change blindness after viewing static displays for a prolonged period of time.

Your answer: ☐

4. Selectively attending to one conversation while ignoring others, but being attentive to self-referent information, was referred to as the cocktail party problem by which psychologist?

    A. Cherry (1953).

    B. Logan (1996).

    C. Broadbent (1958).

    D. Marcel (1983).

Your answer: ☐

5. Which syndrome is associated with fixed gazing, poor ability to reach for objects and simultagnosia?

    A. Broca's.

    B. Cherry's.

    C. Marr's.

    D. Balint's.

Your answer: ☐

6. Allport (1989) argued for the importance of which relationship?

    A. Divided and selective attention.

    B. Focused and impaired attention.

    C. Motivation and attention.

    D. Sensory register and short-term memory.

Your answer: ☐

7. An action which has progressed from being conscious to automatic could be said to have undergone which process?

  A. Proceduralisation.

  B. Transmission.

  C. Generalisation.

  D. Extension.

Your answer: ☐

8. According to the similarity theory, which stimuli are the most difficult to detect?

  A. Target items which are similar to each other.

  B. Target items which are similar to distractors.

  C. Target items which are dissimilar to distractors.

  D. Target items which are dissimilar to each other.

Your answer: ☐

9. Attentional biases have been observed for which type of stimuli?

  A. Threatening stimuli.

  B. Positive stimuli.

  C. Self-referential stimuli.

  D. All of the above.

Your answer: ☐

10. Which theory was proposed as a compromise to those of Broadbent (1958) and Deutsch and Deutsch (1963) and incorporated both early and late selection?

  A. Attenuation theory.

  B. Bottleneck theory.

  C. Perceptual load theory.

  D. Filter theory.

Your answer: ☐

11. Which of the following is not one of Posner and Petersen's (1990) abilities controlling the attentional spotlight?

   A. Disengagement.

   B. Shifting.

   C. Highlighting.

   D. Engaging.

Your answer: ☐

Advanced level questions

12. Which mechanism prevents attending to a visual location repeatedly?

   A. Inhibition of return.

   B. Split attention.

   C. Covert attention.

   D. Visual spotlight.

Your answer: ☐

13. According to Reason (1990), preservations refer to which form of 'slips' in automatic processing?

   A. Preceding sensory information distorts existing processes.

   B. Repetition of an action already performed.

   C. A step or process is unconsciously missed.

   D. Failure to change a course of action.

Your answer: ☐

14. Effortful identification of a particular target stimulus within a dynamic display containing distractors is best achieved using which processes?

   A. Search.

   B. Divided attention.

   C. Selective attention.

   D. Vigilance.

Your answer: ☐

15. Which of the following is true with regard to Broadbent's (1958) theory of attention?

    A. Several channels of information are transmitted through the attenuation control.

    B. It does not incorporate short-term memory.

    C. There is an early and late filter for sensory information.

    D. Only one channel of information is transmitted through the selective filter.

Your answer: ☐

16. Broadbent's (1958) model is also categorised as which of the following?

    A. Late selection model.

    B. Dual selection model.

    C. Early selection model.

    D. Parallel selection model.

Your answer: ☐

17. What is the correct order of attentional processing according to Broadbent's (1958) model?

    A. Stimulus input, sensory memory, filter, perceptual channel and response.

    B. Sensory memory, perceptual channel, filter and response.

    C. Stimulus input, perceptual channel, filter, inner scribe and response.

    D. Stimulus input, filter, perceptual channel, sensory memory and response.

Your answer: ☐

18. In which construct did Treisman (1970) argue attenuation must occur?

    A. Sensory memory.

    B. Central executive.

    C. Filter.

    D. Perceptual channel.

Your answer: ☐

19. According to Treisman's (1970) dictionary unit, which stimuli would contain information converning how activation thresholds facilitate attention to these items?

    A. Words which are distinctive or emotionally charged.

    B. Words which are especially common or personally important.

    C. Words which are not self-referent or emotional.

    D. Words which are uncommon or self-referent.

Your answer: ☐

20. According to the capacity theory of attention, the demands made on the cognitive system by dichotic listening and shadowing would result in which form of attention?

    A. Divided attention and equal consideration of both target stimuli and unattended channels.

    B. Selective attention to target stimuli and no processing of unattended channels.

    C. Short-term attentional biases for threatening stimuli and inhibition of return.

    D. Attentional saturation and fatigue effects for processing all stimuli.

Your answer: ☐

21. Multiple resource theories state that impaired task performance will arise in which circumstance?

    A. When two simultaneous tasks both require high capacity and different resources.

    B. When two simultaneous tasks require different levels of capacity and the same resources.

    C. When two simultaneous tasks require different levels of capacity and different resources.

    D. When two simultaneous tasks both require high capacity and the same resources.

Your answer: ☐

22. Schneider and Shiffrin (1977) observed which pattern of results?

    A. Varied mapping evoked effortful processes, consistent mapping evoked automatic processes.

    B. Varied mapping evoked both effortful and automatic processes.

    C. Consistent mapping and varied mapping evoked effortful processes.

    D. Consistent mapping evoked effortful processing, varied mapping evoked no effect.

Your answer: ☐

23. In which structures did Posner (1995) identify an anterior attentional system and posterior attentional system respectively?

    A. Temporal lobe and hypothalamus.

    B. Amygdala and parietal lobe.

    C. Frontal lobe and parietal lobe.

    D. Left temporal lobe and right temporal lobe.

Your answer: ☐

Extended multiple-choice question

Complete the following representation of Broadbent's (1958) model using the items listed opposite. Not all of the items will be consistent with the model and not all items can be used. Items can be used only once.

- Numerous sources of information are present in the environment.

- Information is processed through the _____ register.

- The _____ filter focuses on one channel of information.

- _____ processes are initiated to process basic features about the stimuli.

- Information is transmitted and stored briefly in _____ memory.

- A _____ is made dependent upon the task and attentional processes.

Optional items

A. attentional control

B. attenuation

C. lexical

D. limited capacity

E. long-term

F. perceptual

G. selective

H. semantic

I. short-term

J. sensory

Essay questions for Chapter 3

Once you have completed the MCQs you are ready to tackle the example essay questions below. You might like to select three or four topics and make notes on them. One way of doing this is to create a concept map. The first question has been done for you and you can see how the knowledge required links to some of the MCQs in this chapter.

1. Critically compare and contrast Broadbent's (1958) filter theory and Treisman's (1960) attenuation theory of attention.

2. Evaluate a minimum of two theories concerning divided attention.

3. Identify, discuss and evaluate evidence for attentional structures in the brain with reference to divided, selective and focused attention.

4. Critically discuss the claim that visual search has contributed more towards understanding attention than other experimental techniques.

5. Critically discuss theoretical accounts and experimental evidence concerning attentional biases.

6. To what extent have neuropsychology and neuroscience contributed towards the study of normal and impaired attention?

7. Critically discuss the methodological advancements in the study of attention.

8. Evaluate the claim that theoretical accounts have guided experimental investigations into the nature of attention.

Chapter 3 essay question 1: concept map

Critically compare and contrast Broadbent's (1958) filter theory and Treisman's (1960) attenuation theory of attention.

The following concept map presents an example of how your responses to this question could be structured in a meaningful and comprehensive way. There are also links to specific questions in this chapter to guide your revision process. The theories presented by Broadbent (1958) and Treisman (1960) are compared and contrasted for their structures, processes and evidence with explicit examples for each of these aspects.

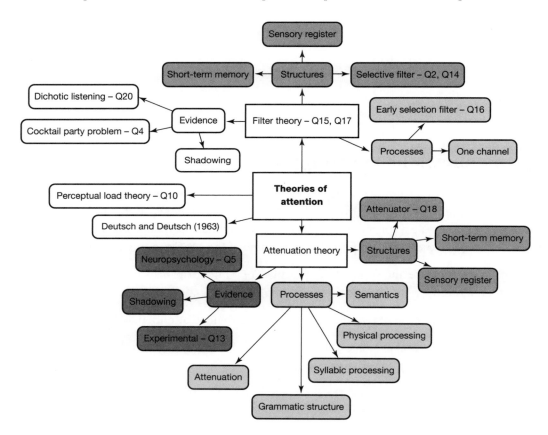

Chapter 4
Models of memory

This chapter provides questions relating to the prominent models of memory. It includes topics such as schools of thought, the scope of the subject, key terms and concepts, methodological considerations and prominent milestones in memory research. It will test both your foundation and advanced knowledge of these topics. At the end of the chapter are several example essay questions and a sample concept map which may enable you to organise your thoughts during essay planning.

Select one answer for each question.

Foundation level questions

1. Memory systems must typically be able to perform which tasks without impairment?

   A. Formulate, calculate and state.

   B. Encode, store and retrieve.

   C. Construct, manipulate and reconstruct.

   D. All of the above.

   Your answer:

2. Which of the terms below refers to auditory sensory memory?

   A. Echoic.

   B. Idiographic.

   C. Iconic.

   D. Masking.

   Your answer:

3. Sperling (1960) presented participants with which form of stimuli?

    A. Words presented verbally.

    B. Words presented visually.

    C. Visual arrays of 12 letters.

    D. Pictures varying in emotional salience.

Your answer:

4. Explicit or declarative memory consists of which information?

    A. Automatic motor skills, episodic, semantic.

    B. Non-automatic motor skills, automatic motor skills, episodic.

    C. Semantic, episodic, autobiographical.

    D. Unconscious memories, autobiographical, conceptual.

Your answer:

5. What is the primary difference between episodic and semantic memory?

    A. Episodic is short term, semantic is long term.

    B. Episodic is declarative, semantic is implicit.

    C. Episodic and semantic are equivalent terms.

    D. Episodic contains information about events, semantic contains facts and concepts.

Your answer:

6. Patient HM's memory deficits were primarily in which form of memory?

    A. Long-term episodic memory.

    B. Long-term procedural memory.

    C. Short-term echoic memory.

    D. Short-term iconic memory.

Your answer:

7. Which cortical structure has been found to play a significant role in storing long-term memories based on patients such as HM?

  A. Amygdala.

  B. Left temporal lobe.

  C. Hippocampus.

  D. Frontal lobe.

Your answer: ☐

8. Which of these measures would be used to assess short-term memory?

  A. Diaries.

  B. Digit span.

  C. Back-propagation.

  D. Map reading.

Your answer: ☐

9. The serial position effect refers to which two effects?

  A. Primacy and recency.

  B. Chunking and recency.

  C. Priming and primacy.

  D. Priming and chunking.

Your answer: ☐

10. Peterson and Peterson (1959) identified that short-term memory typically lasts for how long?

  A. 10 seconds.

  B. 29 seconds.

  C. 5–9 seconds.

  D. 18 seconds.

Your answer: ☐

Advanced level questions

11. Which factor contributes towards a short-term memory being transferred to long-term storage according to the modal model?

    A. Rehearsal.

    B. Successful processing by the central executive.

    C. Levels of processing.

    D. Articulatory suppression.

    Your answer:

12. Which component of Baddeley and Hitch's (1974) model is responsible for storing speech-like information in the short-term?

    A. Sketch pad.

    B. Phonological loop.

    C. Central executive.

    D. Sensory store.

    Your answer:

13. Which of the following is not attributed to the central executive in working memory?

    A. Supervisory control.

    B. Focus and switch attention.

    C. Maintain active memory using inner speech.

    D. Retrieve representations from long-term memory.

    Your answer:

14. Which of the psychologists below formulated the theory concerning the 'inner scribe'?

    A. Baddeley and Hitch (1974).

    B. Atkinson and Shiffrin (1971).

    C. McClelland (1991).

    D. Logie (1995).

    Your answer:

15. According to Baddeley's (2000) multi-component model, which of the following are in the category of crystallised systems?

   A. Episodic buffer, visual semantics, language.

   B. Language, visual semantics, episodic long-term memory.

   C. Visuo-spatial sketch pad, episodic buffer, inner scribe.

   D. Central executive, visual semantics, inner scribe.

Your answer: ☐

16. Collins and Quillian (1969) devised which type of model for semantic memory?

   A. A spreading activation model.

   B. The dual-route model.

   C. A multi-store model.

   D. A connectionist model.

Your answer: ☐

17. According to Craik and Tulving (1975), which of these options demonstrates increasing depth?

   A. Physical, semantic, phonological.

   B. Physical, phonological, semantic.

   C. Semantic, phonological, physical.

   D. Phonological, physical, semantic.

Your answer: ☐

18. Connectionist models have been used to simulate and explore which aspects of memory?

   A. Learning, semantics, associations, implicit memory.

   B. Impairment, interference, damage, explicit memory.

   C. Conceptual knowledge, memory for faces, phonological processing.

   D. All of the above.

Your answer: ☐

19. McClelland and Rumelhart (1985) demonstrated that a distributed model could function as if it had acquired which of the following?

A. Anatomical structures and heuristics.

B. Autobiographical and flashbulb memories.

C. Prototypes, logogens and rules.

D. Independent functions and anatomical structures.

Your answer: ☐

20. In which component of connectionist networks would the computational equivalent of cognition occur?

A. Hidden units and connections.

B. Input units and output units.

C. Short-term and long-term memory.

D. Connections and output units.

Your answer: ☐

Extended multiple-choice question

Complete the following multi-component working memory model using the items listed opposite.

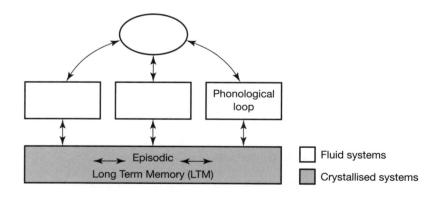

Optional items

A. Attenuator

B. Central executive

C. Episodic buffer

D. Language

E. Perceptual loop

F. Rehearsal extender

G. Semantic buffer

H. Tactile processing

I. Visual semantics

J. Visuospatial sketchpad

Essay questions for Chapter 4

Once you have completed the MCQs you are ready to tackle the example essay questions below. You might like to select three or four topics and make notes on them. One way of doing this is to create a concept map. The first question has been done for you and you can see how the knowledge required links to some of the MCQs in this chapter.

1. Compare and contrast the modal model and working memory model of memory.

2. Evaluate the contemporary relevance of the working memory model with reference to research with both healthy and neuropsychological participants.

3. Critically evaluate traditional and connectionist approaches to studying memory.

4. To what extent have traditional and contemporary research contributed towards identifying which of the models of memory are the most accurate?

5. Discuss the extent to which theory has guided practice with reference to models of memory.

6. Compare and contrast connectionist and symbolic models of memory.

7. Evaluate the contributions of connectionist modelling to theories and research concerning the nature of memory.

8. Discuss and evaluate the methodological advancements which have emerged during the study of memory.

Chapter 4 essay question 1: concept map

Compare and contrast the modal model and working memory model of memory.

The following concept map presents an example of how your responses to this question could be structured in a meaningful and comprehensive way. There are also links to specific questions in this chapter to guide your revision process. The working memory model and modal model are compared and contrasted with reference to the research evidence, systems, structures and processes with explicit examples for each of these aspects.

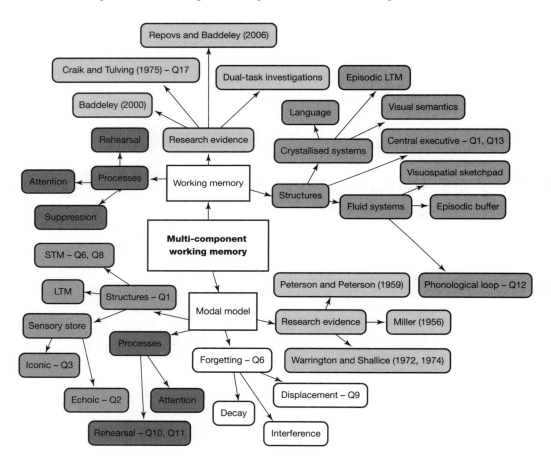

Chapter 5
Applied aspects of memory

This chapter provides questions relating to applied aspects of memory. It includes topics such as schools of thought, the scope of the subject, key terms and concepts, methodological considerations and prominent milestones in applied memory research. It will test both your foundation and advanced knowledge of these topics. At the end of the chapter are several example essay questions and a sample concept map which may enable you to organise your thoughts during essay planning.

Select one answer for each question.

Foundation level questions

1. What is the primary advantage to studying memory in real-world situations?

    A. Increased experimental control.

    B. No interpretation biases.

    C. Increased ecological validity.

    D. Facilitates connectionist modelling.

    Your answer: ☐

2. Bransford and Johnson (1973) demonstrated that memory can be which of the following?

    A. Reconstructive.

    B. Constructive.

    C. Suggestible.

    D. Discriminatory.

    Your answer: ☐

3. Watkins and Tulving (1975) demonstrated which phenomenon?

    A. Schema distortions.

    B. Encoding-specificity.

    C. Weapons effects.

    D. Flashbulb memories.

Your answer: ☐

4. How many sins of memory were identified by Schacter (2001)?

    A. 3.

    B. 10.

    C. 5.

    D. 7.

Your answer: ☐

5. The tip of the tongue phenomenon reflects which sin of memory?

    A. Blocking.

    B. Transience.

    C. Misattribution.

    D. Persistence.

Your answer: ☐

6. Suggestibility can be demonstrated using which of the following?

    A. Stroop.

    B. Diary studies.

    C. Leading questions.

    D. Free association.

Your answer: ☐

7. Amnesia usually reflects the loss of which form of memory?

   A. Procedural.

   B. Explicit.

   C. Implicit.

   D. Tacit.

Your answer: ☐

8. What did Wells (1993) argue was the leading factor for wrongful convictions?

   A. Eyewitness testimony.

   B. Judge's forgetfulness.

   C. Defence attorney's misattribution.

   D. Poor autobiographical memory.

Your answer: ☐

9. Spear (1979) observed which form of memory loss?

   A. Alzheimer's disease.

   B. Anterograde amnesia.

   C. Infantile amnesia.

   D. Retrograde amnesia.

Your answer: ☐

10. Which of the following may explain evidence concerning validity of eyewitness reports?

   A. Constructive memory.

   B. Suggestibility.

   C. Demand characteristics.

   D. All of the above.

Your answer: ☐

11. Who identified that the selection of an individual from a line-up could be biased by the other individuals present?

    A. Berkowitz, Laney, Morris, Garry and Loftus (2008).

    B. Wells, Luus and Windschitl (1994).

    C. Loftus (2005).

    D. Dolan (1996).

Your answer: ☐

Advanced level questions

12. According to Payne et al. (2002), what is the typical effect of stress on recall and identification?

    A. Both decline.

    B. Both improve.

    C. Recall increases, identification is unchanged.

    D. Identification declines, recall improves.

Your answer: ☐

13. Ceci and Bruck (1993, 1995) observed that children's memory was especially prone to which of the following?

    A. Distortion.

    B. Emotionality.

    C. Trauma.

    D. Repression.

Your answer: ☐

14. Which of the techniques below can be used to improve eyewitness testimony?

    A. Experimentation.

    B. Memory training.

    C. Cognitive interviews.

    D. Introducing weapons effects.

Your answer: ☐

15. The tendency for repressed memories to only surface after the onset of therapy potentially due to therapist suggestion is known as which of the following?

A. Isotopic.

B. Iatrogenic.

C. Dissociative.

D. Reconstructive.

Your answer: ☐

16. Flashbulb memories are believed to form given which circumstances?

A. When the context at retrieval is the same as at storage.

B. When the mood at retrieval is the same as at storage.

C. When events are personally salient but not emotional.

D. When events are emotionally charged, highly publicised and distinctive.

Your answer: ☐

17. Prospective memory refers to which of the following?

A. Remembering friends from primary school.

B. Remembering the categories of objects.

C. Remembering to perform an intended task.

D. Remembering how to play a game.

Your answer: ☐

18. Warren and Haslam (2007) observed overgeneralisation for public and autobiographical memories in which clinical groups?

A. Patients with Alzheimer's or semantic dementia.

B. Patients with depression or schizophrenia.

C. Patients with social or personality disorders.

D. Patients with developmental impairment or dissociative identity disorder.

Your answer: ☐

19. What is the primary difference between self-monitoring and self-regulation?

    A. Self-monitoring is a bottom-up process, self-regulation is a top-down process.

    B. Self-monitoring is a top-down process, self-regulation is a bottom-up process.

    C. Self-regulation is performed by children, self-monitoring is performed by adults.

    D. None of these, they are equivalent terms.

Your answer: ☐

20. Diary studies can be used to access which form of memory?

    A. Procedural.

    B. Implicit.

    C. Autobiographic.

    D. Sensory.

Your answer: ☐

21. Belmont and Butterfield (1971) identified that which technique could aid memory in children with mental retardation?

    A. Rehearsal training.

    B. Imagination.

    C. Method of loci.

    D. Transposition.

Your answer: ☐

Extended multiple-choice question

Complete the following paragraph using the items listed below. Not all of the items will be consistent with the paragraph and not all items can be used. Items can be used only once.

_____ employed the method of _____ and demonstrated the reconstructive nature of memory. This technique includes copying a drawing from memory or recounting a story in the same format. Participants often reconstruct elements of the story or drawing to make it consistent with their own _____ and personal expectations irrespective of the actual items encountered during the task. Bartlett (1932) theorised that the memory distortions observed using this task arise due to the influence of schemata. However, schema theory originated in the work by _____ . _____ demonstrated how reconstructive memory and leading questions can also influence the accuracy of eyewitness testimony. A second example of how schemas may influence recall is demonstrated by _____. This refers to the phenomenon in which participants combine elements of a story or fill in the gaps in their memory with plausible alternatives in states of high motivation and emotion.

Optional items

A. Baddeley (2001)

B. Bartlett (1932)

C. confabulation

D. cultural

E. eyewitness testimony

F. Piaget (1926)

G. Loftus and Palmer (1974)

H. neuropsychology

I. reiteration

J. serial reproduction

Essay questions for Chapter 5

Once you have completed the MCQs you are ready to tackle the example essay questions below. You might like to select three or four topics and make notes on them. One way of doing this is to create a concept map. The first question has been done for you and you can see how the knowledge required links to some of the MCQs in this chapter.

1. Critically discuss and compare the advantages and disadvantages of studying memory within experimental and real-world settings.

2. Evaluate the contributions of research investigating the validity of eyewitness testimony towards a broad understanding of memory.

3. Discuss the claim that the constructive, reconstructive and suggestible nature of memory prevents accurate storage, retrieval and production.

4. To what extent has neuropsychology and the use of case studies expanded the understanding of applied aspects of memory?

5. Evaluate the extent to which the study of prospective memory demonstrates the importance of understanding the applied aspects of memory.

6. Critically discuss the validity and reliability of research demonstrating the reconstructive nature of memory in real-world situations.

7. Evaluate the extent to which experimental techniques can be applied to study memory in more ecologically valid settings.

8. Critically discuss evidence for and against flashbulb memories.

Chapter 5 essay question 1: concept map

Critically discuss and compare the advantages and disadvantages of studying memory within experimental and real-world settings.

The following concept map presents an example of how your responses to this question could be structured in a meaningful and comprehensive way. There are also links to specific questions in this chapter to guide your revision process. The advantages, disadvantages and areas of study associated with real world, and various experimental approaches are compared and contrasted with reference to explicit examples for each of these aspects of your response.

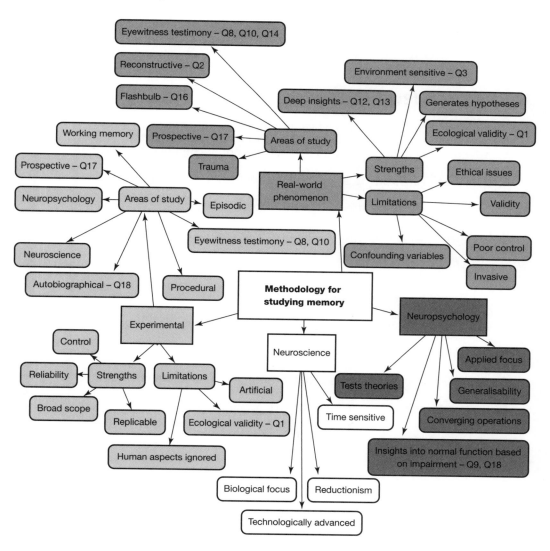

Chapter 6
Cognition and emotion

This chapter provides questions relating to the interaction between cognition and emotion. It includes topics such as schools of thought, the scope of the subject, key terms and concepts, methodological considerations and prominent milestones in applied memory research. It will test both your foundation and advanced knowledge of these topics. At the end of the chapter are several example essay questions and a sample concept map which may enable you to organise your thoughts during essay planning.

Select one answer for each question.

Foundation level questions

1. Zajonc (1984, 1989) advocated which of the following views?

    A. Affective evaluation of stimuli can occur without cognitive processing.

    B. Cognitive processing is essential for affective evaluation of stimuli.

    C. Schemas determine affective evaluation of stimuli.

    D. State and trait anxiety guide cognitive processing.

    Your answer: ☐

2. Lazarus (1982) advocated which of the following views?

    A. Affective evaluation of stimuli can occur without cognitive processing.

    B. Schemas determine affective evaluation of stimuli.

    C. Cognitive processing is essential for affective evaluation of stimuli.

    D. State and trait anxiety guide cognitive processing.

    Your answer: ☐

3. Which of the following stages is not a level included in Lazarus's (1982) theory?

   A. Primary appraisal.

   B. Pre-appraisal.

   C. Secondary appraisal.

   D. Re-appraisal.

Your answer: ☐

4. Zajonc (1980) cited the mere exposure effect as support for which theory?

   A. Affective primacy hypothesis.

   B. Cognitive appraisal.

   C. Mood-state theory.

   D. Schema theory.

Your answer: ☐

5. Lazarus (1982) observed that which of the following reduced stress?

   A. Imageability and familiarity.

   B. Frequency of exposure and denial.

   C. Affective primacy and familiarity.

   D. Denial and intellectualisations.

Your answer: ☐

6. Which of the following is not included in the SPAARS model?

   A. Analogical system.

   B. Appraisal system.

   C. Schematic system.

   D. Associative system.

Your answer: ☐

7. Which of the following is not an aspect of Smith and Lazarus's (1993) secondary appraisal?

A. Problem-focused coping potential.

B. Emotion-focused coping potential.

C. Motivational relevance.

D. Future expectancy.

Your answer:

8. Which two structures relay emotional information according to the fast circuit advocated by LeDoux (1992, 1996)?

A. Hypothalamus and frontal lobe.

B. Thalamus and amygdala.

C. Left temporal lobe and hypothalamus.

D. Hypothalamus and amygdala.

Your answer:

9. LeDoux's (1992, 1996) slow circuit incorporates which of the following?

A. Noradrenaline.

B. Serotonin.

C. Motivational congruence.

D. Cortex.

Your answer:

10. Gilligan and Bower (1984) modelled emotions as which of the following?

A. Nodes in a semantic network.

B. Schemas.

C. Automatic and meaning free.

D. Propositional systems.

Your answer:

11. The tendency for recall to improve when participants' mood is similar during learning and testing is known as which of the following?

    A. Mood congruency.

    B. Thought congruency.

    C. Mood-state dependent.

    D. Mood intensity.

Your answer: ☐

Advanced level questions

12. According to the schema theory, which stimuli would participants with phobias process faster?

    A. Phobia-congruent items.

    B. Phobia-incongruent items.

    C. Low-intensity stimuli.

    D. None of the above.

Your answer: ☐

13. Graf and Mandler (1984) drew a distinction between which two techniques?

    A. Visual search and dot-probe.

    B. Elaboration and dot-probe.

    C. Visual search and priming.

    D. Priming and elaboration.

Your answer: ☐

14. Williams et al. (1988) argued that depressed patients should demonstrate which of the following?

    A. Implicit memory bias for threatening information.

    B. Procedural memory bias for unpleasant experiences.

    C. Explicit memory bias for threatening information.

    D. Priming effects for threatening information.

Your answer: ☐

15. Williams et al. (1988) argued that anxious patients should demonstrate which of the following?

    A. Explicit memory bias for threatening information.

    B. Implicit memory bias for threatening information.

    C. Procedural memory bias for unpleasant experiences.

    D. Priming effects for threatening information.

Your answer:

16. Which of the following is not one of Rusting's (1998) ways in which emotional processing can be influenced by traits and states?

    A. Traditional.

    B. Mediator.

    C. Moderator.

    D. Contemporary.

Your answer:

17. Bower et al. (1978) observed mood-state dependent memory in which of the following?

    A. Two-list design.

    B. One-list design.

    C. Emotional stroop.

    D. Priming.

Your answer:

18. Ucros (1989) observed that mood-state dependent memory is more pronounced in which state?

    A. Negative.

    B. Positive.

    C. Neutral.

    D. Intoxicated.

Your answer:

19. What tool did Bower et al. (1981) employ to induce mood states?

    A. Antagonism.

    B. Cortical electrical stimulation.

    C. Hypnotism.

    D. Pharmaceuticals.

Your answer: ☐

20. Perrig and Perrig (1981) observed that mood-congruent effects could occur using which of the following?

    A. Electrical stimulation and mood induction.

    B. Mood induction and mood simulation.

    C. Mood simulation and priming.

    D. Hypnotism and electrical stimulation.

Your answer: ☐

21. The argument that mood states influence internal events more than external events was advocated by which of the following?

    A. Beck (1976).

    B. Bower (1980).

    C. Rusting (1998).

    D. Eich and Metcalfe (1989).

Your answer: ☐

22. In the case of anxiety, interpretive bias refers to which phenomenon?

    A. Ambiguous stimuli are interpreted as threatening.

    B. Attention is directed towards threatening stimuli.

    C. The visual spotlight automatically focuses on threatening stimuli.

    D. Hypervigilence for threatening stimuli.

Your answer: ☐

Extended multiple-choice question

Complete the following paragraph using the items listed below. Not all of the items will be consistent with the paragraph and not all items can be used. Items can be used only once.

The study of emotion and cognition demonstrates a significant example of how numerous schools of thought have attempted to describe phenomena. For example, from a _____ perspective, _____ argued that emotions set the _____ of any intelligent being and are therefore extrinsically linked to cognition. Indeed, emotional responses can determine, or be in response to, cognitive _____, thought, goals and actions. However, _____ theories also state that some behaviours and responses may be determined by reflexes which benefit the organism's chances of survival. For example, in the case of threatening stimuli, the startle response may arise rapidly and without conscious appraisal. Furthermore, the behaviourist school of thought would suggest that the associations formed during this process could account for anxiety and phobias.

Optional items

A. appraisal

B. behaviourist

C. cognitive

D. evaluation

E. evolutionary

F. humanistic

G. Lazarus (1982)

H. reflexes

I. Simon (1967)

J. priorities

Essay questions for Chapter 6

Once you have completed the MCQs you are ready to tackle the example essay questions below. You might like to select three or four topics and make notes on them. One way of doing this is to create a concept map. The first question has been done for you and you can see how the knowledge required links to some of the MCQs in this chapter.

1. Compare and contrast Zajonc's (1980) and Lazarus's (1982, 1991) accounts of emotion and cognition.

2. Critically evaluate the claim that attentional and interpretive biases are only observed for stimuli with negative valence.

3. Compare and contrast the effects of depression and anxiety on cognitive processing.

4. To what extent have psychopharmacology and neuropsychology contributed towards understanding the relationship between emotion and cognition?

5. Critically discuss the validity and reliability of experimental research investigating the relationship between cognition and emotion.

6. To what extent has the relationship between emotion and cognition been clarified by experimental cognitive psychology?

7. Critically evaluate the SPAARS model with reference to both theory and research.

8. To what extent has Rusting (1998) accounted for the ways in which mood states and trait can influence emotional processing?

Chapter 6 essay question 1: concept map

Compare and contrast Zajonc's (1980) and Lazarus's (1982, 1991) accounts of emotion and cognition.

The following concept map presents an example of how your responses to this question could be structured in a meaningful and comprehensive way. There are also links to specific questions in this chapter to guide your revision process. The theories presented by Zajonc (1980) and Lazarus (1982, 1991) are compared and contrasted with reference to each aspect of these theories.

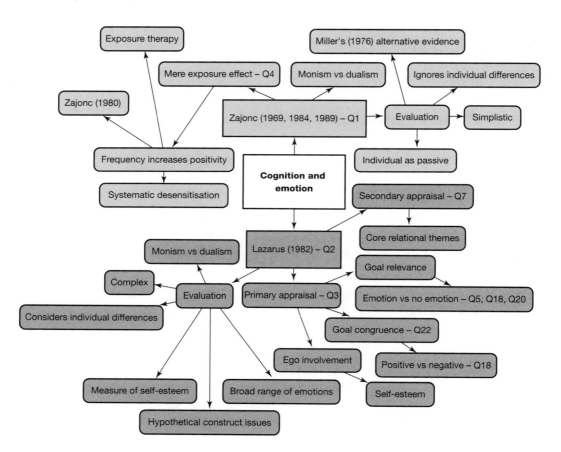

Chapter 7
Cognitive neuropsychology

This chapter provides questions relating to aspects of cognitive neuropsychology. It includes topics such as schools of thought, the scope of the subject, core terms and concepts, methodological considerations and prominent milestones in applied memory research. It will test both your foundation and advanced knowledge of these topics. At the end of the chapter are several example essay questions and a sample concept map which may enable you to organise your thoughts during essay planning.

Select one answer for each question.

Foundation level questions

1. Cognitive neuropsychology typically uses which of the sampling groups below?

   A. Patients with brain damage and neurological conditions.

   B. Participants who excel in an area of expertise.

   C. University students.

   D. None of the above.

   Your answer: ☐

2. Which of the following findings can be used to indicate specialism in a cortical region?

   A. Single dissociation.

   B. Matched performance.

   C. Double dissociation.

   D. Cohorts.

   Your answer: ☐

3. Which of the following is true with regard to cognitive neuropsychology?

    A. It attempts to understand impairment and is not interested in normal function.

    B. It only uses imaging techniques to understand normal functioning.

    C. It never uses case studies or small samples.

    D. It attempts to understand normal function by studying impairment.

Your answer: ☐

4. Coltheart (2001) suggested which interpretation of the deficits shown by patient AC?

    A. There is only one system responsible for object recognition.

    B. There are multiple memory stores.

    C. There are several systems for object recognition, not a singular system.

    D. There are at least three routes to language.

Your answer: ☐

5. Which of the following is usually overlooked in studies from cognitive neuropsychology?

    A. Baseline measures obtained prior to impairment.

    B. Isolation of functions in one cortical region.

    C. Isolation of damage to one cortical structure.

    D. All of the above.

Your answer: ☐

6. Which of the following is rarely used in conjunction with cognitive neuropsychology?

    A. Discourse analysis.

    B. Traditional experimentation.

    C. Neuroimaging.

    D. Cohort studies.

Your answer: ☐

7. Duncan and Owen (2000) presented which of the following arguments?

   A. The hypothalamus displays anatomical modularity.

   B. The frontal lobes are active during multiple tasks.

   C. The frontal lobes display anatomical modularity.

   D. The hippocampus is active during multiple tasks.

Your answer: ☐

8. The assumption that cortical regions function similarly across individuals corresponds to which of the terms below?

   A. Anatomical modularity.

   B. Functional modularity.

   C. Subtractivity of function.

   D. Uniformity of function.

Your answer: ☐

9. Which of the following are double dissociations unable to demonstrate?

   A. More than two systems which are associated with a form of processing.

   B. Two systems in any system of knowledge.

   C. Differential performance by two patients with brain damage.

   D. Unimpaired performance on certain specialised tasks.

Your answer: ☐

10. Shallice (1991) presented which of the following critiques of neuropsychology?

   A. Performance may only reflect the patient's idiosyncratic strategies.

   B. Performance may only demonstrate how the system reorganises functions.

   C. Performance may be dependent on the difficulty of the task.

   D. All of the above.

Your answer: ☐

11. Banich (1997) argued that inferring functional modularity is hindered by which of the following?

    A. Limitations of case studies.

    B. Limitations of group studies.

    C. Interconnectivity of the brain.

    D. Cortical changes occur during the period of rehabilitation.

Your answer: ☐

12. Lesions to which cortical structure can impair emotional responses, emotional memory and the ability to learn conditioned responses?

    A. Hypothalamus.

    B. Amygdala.

    C. Hippocampus.

    D. Basal ganglia.

Your answer: ☐

13. The case of Phineas Gage demonstrates that damage to which cortical structure can reduce inhibition and increase impulsivity and aggression?

    A. Orbitofrontal cortex.

    B. Left temporal lobe.

    C. Right temporal lobe.

    D. Brain stem.

Your answer: ☐

Advanced level questions

14. According to Bechara et al. (1997, 1999), ventromedial prefrontal lesions produced which of the following reactions?

    A. No emotional response to logical and illogical actions.

    B. An emotional response was only displayed prior to demonstrating poor judgements.

    C. An emotional response was displayed both before and after poor judgements were made.

    D. Little ability to guide decision-making but emotional response displayed afterwards.

Your answer: ☐

15. Volitional facial paresis is associated with damage to which of the following regions?

    A. Occipital lobe.

    B. Primary motor cortex.

    C. Basal ganglia.

    D. Cingulate gyrus.

Your answer: ☐

16. Emotional facial paralysis is associated with damage to which of the following regions?

    A. Primary motor cortex and hippocampus.

    B. Amygdala, basal ganglia and occipital lobe.

    C. Prefrontal cortex, frontal lobe and thalamus.

    D. Left temporal lobe, thalamus and hypothalamus.

Your answer: ☐

17. Which of the following patterns of impairment are displayed by patients with Wernicke's aphasia?

   A. Incoherent speech but verbal tone moderated by emotion.

   B. Speech and emotional responses are both incoherent.

   C. Emotional responses are impaired but speech remains intact.

   D. None of the above.

Your answer: ☐

18. On which task did patients with Parkinson's disease perform poorly according to research undertaken by Knowlton, Mangels and Squire (1996)?

   A. Word associates.

   B. Free recall.

   C. Priming.

   D. Probability judgements.

Your answer: ☐

19. Korsakoff's syndrome is a form of which type of amnesia?

   A. Retrograde.

   B. Anterograde.

   C. Retrograde and autobiographical.

   D. Semantic and retrograde.

Your answer: ☐

20. The study of patient HM provided which of the following insights?

   A. The hippocampus is not responsible for long-term memory.

   B. The hippocampus facilitates the transition from short-term to long-term memory.

   C. The hippocampus is not responsible for short-term memory.

   D. All of the above.

Your answer: ☐

21. Which of the following is true with regard to patients WC and SM?

    A. Both displayed damage to the amygdala and impaired conditioned responses.

    B. Both displayed damage to the hippocampus and unimpaired conditioned responses.

    C. Damage to the hippocampus and damage to the amygdala respectively.

    D. Neither displayed impaired conditioned responses but both had a damaged amygdala.

Your answer: ☐

22. Vargha-Khadem et al. (1997) demonstrated that three patients with severe anterograde amnesia displayed which of the patterns below?

    A. Ability to learn factual details, anterograde amnesia for episodic information.

    B. Co-occurring retrograde amnesia.

    C. Ability to learn new episodic information, impaired factual knowledge.

    D. Identical semantic and episodic impairment.

Your answer: ☐

23. Damage to patient RS's left medial temporal lobe and right hippocampus produced which of the following impairments?

    A. Semantic dementia and anterograde amnesia for procedural knowledge.

    B. Retrograde and anterograde amnesia for episodic memory.

    C. Retrograde amnesia for semantic memory.

    D. Korsakoff's syndrome and impaired procedural memory.

Your answer: ☐

24. Which of the following patients displayed semantic dementia?

    A. RS

    B. HM

    C. Clive Wearing

    D. AM

Your answer: ☐

25. Conduction aphasia is consistent with which of the following definitions?

    A. Poor comprehension but average fluent speech.

    B. Incoherent speech but average comprehension.

    C. Unimpaired speech, average comprehension but poor repetition.

    D. Meaningless speech, poor comprehension and poor repetition.

Your answer: ☐

26. The loss of the ability to read without the loss of the ability to write is known as which of the following neuropsychological conditions?

    A. Pure alexia.

    B. Pure aphasia.

    C. Secondary apraxia.

    D. Secondary anomic aphasia.

Your answer: ☐

Extended multiple-choice question

Complete the following paragraph using the items listed opposite. Not all of the items will be consistent with the paragraph and not all items can be used. Items can be used only once.

Cognitive neuropsychology investigates normal and impaired cognitive functioning using a wide variety of experimental techniques. These can include detailed _____ of neurologically impaired patients and _____ in which the performance of matched unimpaired and impaired participants are compared. Hence, traditional experimental techniques, advanced technology and observation are often combined. For example, _____ techniques can be used to identify the cerebral structures and activity associated with specific tasks and forms of cognition. _____ can be used to identify the change in blood flow and oxygenation associated with neural activity. In contrast _____ can be used to produce a three-dimensional image reflecting cerebral structures and activity using a positron-emitting radionuclide. A range of traditional experimental techniques have also been developed, including measures of memory and perceptual and linguistic processing.

Optional items

A. atomic

B. case studies

C. cohort studies

D. event-related potentials

E. functional magnetic resonance imaging

F. galvanic skin response

G. neuroimaging

H. neuroscience

I. positron emission tomography

J. twin studies

Essay questions for Chapter 7

Once you have completed the MCQs you are ready to tackle the example essay questions below. You might like to select three or four topics and make notes on them. One way of doing this is to create a concept map. The first question has been done for you and you can see how the knowledge required links to some of the MCQs in this chapter.

1. Critically evaluate the contributions made by cognitive neuropsychology towards the understanding of memory and language.

2. To what extent have studies in cognitive neuropsychology presented valid, reliable and replicable findings? Discuss with reference to a minimum of two areas of cognitive psychology.

3. To what extent can contemporary cognitive neuropsychology be considered to be an independent and self-sufficient branch of psychology?

4. Critically evaluate the strengths and limitations of methodologies available to researchers in cognitive neuropsychology.

5. Compare and contrast the insights provided by research using neurologically healthy participants and neurologically impaired patients with reference to memory and perception.

6. Critically discuss the claim that case studies in neuropsychology present fewer insights into normal cognition than those provided by traditional experimental research and cognitive neuroscience.

7. Critically evaluate the strengths, limitations and challenges produced when conducting research with neurologically impaired patients.

8. To what extent has cognitive neuropsychology expanded and clarified understandings concerning the function and structure of the brain? Discuss with reference to Coltheart's (2001) assumptions of cognitive neuropsychology.

Chapter 7 essay question 1: concept map

Critically evaluate the contributions made by cognitive neuropsychology towards the understanding of memory and language.

The following concept map presents an example of how your responses to this question could be structured in a meaningful and comprehensive way. There are also links to specific questions in this chapter to guide your revision process. The contributions made by cognitive neuropsychology towards an understanding of memory and language are presented and evaluated with reference to alternative insights, strengths and limitations.

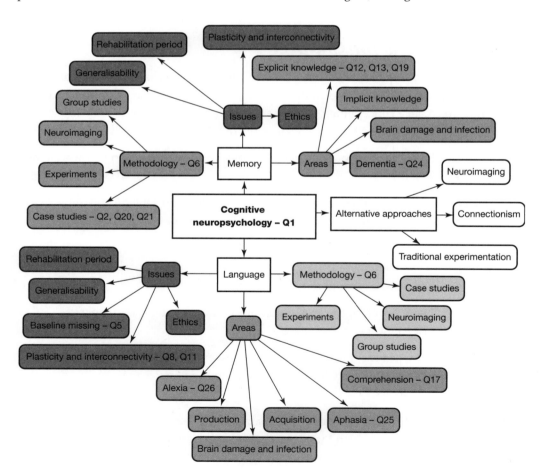

Chapter 8
Language

This chapter provides questions relating to language acquisition, comprehension and production. It includes topics such as schools of thought, the scope of the subject, core concepts, methodological considerations and prominent milestones in research. It will test both your foundation and advanced knowledge of these topics. At the end of the chapter are several example essay questions and a sample concept map which may enable you to organise your thoughts during essay planning.

Select one answer for each question.

Foundation level questions

1. Which of the following can be expressed through language?

    A. Feelings.

    B. Thoughts.

    C. Experiences.

    D. All of the above.

    Your answer: ☐

2. Which subject investigates the interaction between language and thought?

    A. Paralinguistics.

    B. Psycholinguistics.

    C. Animal linguistics.

    D. Symbolic linguistics.

    Your answer: ☐

3. The principle that language is generative and productive refers to which of the following points?

   A. The possibility of creating completely new utterances.

   B. Linguistic structure is observed at both a micro and a macro level.

   C. Language is a coherent and shared system.

   D. Thought is not possible without a system of symbols.

Your answer: ☐

4. The term coarticulation refers to which of the following?

   A. Overlap of phonemes.

   B. Overlap of morphemes.

   C. Overlap of syllables.

   D. Overlap of lexemes.

Your answer: ☐

5. At what age do children in every culture usually start to babble?

   A. 3 years.

   B. 4 months.

   C. 7 months.

   D. 2 years.

Your answer: ☐

6. Which of the following is true for newborns?

   A. Preference for mother's voice rather than strangers' voices.

   B. Preference for native speech rather than other languages.

   C. Emotional expressions of newborns match caregivers' expressions.

   D. All of the above.

Your answer: ☐

7. Which of the following influence language comprehension?

   A. Word frequency and age of acquisition.

   B. Contexts and priming.

   C. Lexical ambiguity and word frequency.

   D. All of the above.

Your answer: ☐

8. Which theoretical structure hypothetically stores all linguistic information?

   A. Schemata.

   B. Mental lexicon.

   C. Mental maps.

   D. Phonological loop.

Your answer: ☐

9. What is the shortest segment of speech which alters the meaning of the word if changed?

   A. Morpheme.

   B. Grapheme.

   C. Phoneme.

   D. Lexeme.

Your answer: ☐

10. Chomsky (1957) argued that the drive to acquire language was which of the following?

   A. Genetically programmed.

   B. Socially constructed.

   C. Established by operant conditioning.

   D. Culturally variable.

Your answer: ☐

11. The abbreviation LAD in psycholinguistics refers to which of the following?

   A. Linguistic-acquisition delay.

   B. Language-acquisition density.

   C. Language-acquisition device.

   D. Language-atrophy device.

Your answer: ☐

12. Which of the following words contains two morphemes?

   A. Table.

   B. Cupboard.

   C. Chair.

   D. Kitchen.

Your answer: ☐

13. Rules which govern the combination of words into sentences are termed which of the following?

   A. Semantics.

   B. Lexicons.

   C. Logogens.

   D. Syntax.

Your answer: ☐

14. Parsing performs which of the following functions?

   A. Organising rhyming items based on corresponding syllables.

   B. Identifying the message of a sentence based on the meaning of the words.

   C. Clarifying the meaning of single words based on conceptual knowledge.

   D. None of the above.

Your answer: ☐

15. What occurs in the case of subtractive bilingualism?

A. The second language completely replaces the first language.

B. Both the first and second languages are acquired from birth but one becomes dominant.

C. Elements of the second language replace elements of the first language.

D. The first language blocks any attempt to learn a second language.

Your answer: ☐

Advanced level questions

16. Speech segmentation is consistent with which of these definitions?

A. The ability to clearly perceive separate words in a stream of speech.

B. The ability to clearly articulate separate words in a stream of speech.

C. The ability to clearly encode separate words from text.

D. The ability to clearly segment individual words into meaningless utterances.

Your answer: ☐

17. Syntax and semantics are considered to be influential factors in which of these theories?

A. Garden-path model of parsing.

B. Syntax-first approach to parsing.

C. Behaviourist approach to parsing.

D. Interactionist approach to parsing.

Your answer: ☐

18. Activation of the N400 event-related potential is taken to mean which of the following?

A. Lexical processing.

B. Semantic processing.

C. Phonological processing.

D. Perceptual processing.

Your answer: ☐

19. Synchrony between visual and auditory information was observed by which of the researchers below?

A. Carroll (1986).

B. Butterworth and Howard (1987).

C. McGurk and MacDonald (1976).

D. Pinker (1999).

Your answer: ☐

20. Rubin et al. (1980) identified which pattern of differences?

A. Girls preferred to discuss sources of personal pride, boys preferred to discuss fears.

B. Girls preferred to discuss feelings, boys preferred to discuss political views.

C. Girls preferred to discuss fears, boys preferred to discuss emotions.

D. Girls preferred to discuss feelings towards people, boys preferred to discuss fears.

Your answer: ☐

21. What is the term assigned to inferences which link an object in one sentence to an object in another sentence?

A. Anaphoric.

B. Instrumental.

C. Causal.

D. Metaphorical.

Your answer: ☐

22. Activation of the P600 event-related potential reflects which of the following?

A. Violations in semantics.

B. Violations in phonology.

C. Violations in morphemes.

D. Violations in syntax.

Your answer: ☐

23. Late closure refers to which of the following definitions?

    A. Overgeneralisation displayed by children during language acquisition.

    B. Overly long sentences produced when the participant is anxious.

    C. Assuming a new word is part of the current phrase.

    D. Ignoring syntax and over-relying on meaning.

Your answer: ☐

24. With regard to bilingualism, proponents of which account would argue the first and second languages are represented in separate systems?

    A. Dual system.

    B. Single system.

    C. Multiple system.

    D. Bilateral system.

Your answer: ☐

25. Savage-Rumbaugh and Lewin (1994) demonstrated which of the following phenomena?

    A. Cultural differences in language acquisition, production and comprehension.

    B. Ability of a chimpanzee to acquire a language system.

    C. Socio-economic differences in language acquisition, production and comprehension.

    D. Birds produce an automatic and universal system of communication.

Your answer: ☐

26. If a similar phoneme is exchanged between one word and another and the replaced phoneme is relocated to the second word, this is an example of which of the following?

    A. Word substitution.

    B. Freudian slip.

    C. Syntactic-category rule.

    D. Consonant-vowel rule.

Your answer: ☐

27. Sentences constructed using both information the listener knows and new information in conversation is consistent with which of the following?

   A. Syntactic priming.

   B. Given-new contract.

   C. Semantic priming.

   D. Concept-syntax rule.

Your answer: ☐

28. What term is given to a speech act in which a person expresses a belief that a proposition is true?

   A. Directive.

   B. Commissive.

   C. Representative.

   D. Expressive.

Your answer: ☐

29. The term 'maxim of relation' refers to which of the following?

   A. Contributions made to a conversation should be consistent with the aims of that conversation.

   B. Meaning should be shared by all participants in a conversation.

   C. Participants in a conversation should build trust and familiarity.

   D. The rules learnt for a first language should be transferable to the intended second language.

Your answer: ☐

30. Which of the following is consistent with the Sapir-Whorf hypothesis?

   A. Individuals' language is influenced by their culture's thought.

   B. Thought processes do not vary across cultures.

   C. Individuals' cognition is influenced by their culture's language.

   D. Men and women vary in their ability to acquire language.

Your answer: ☐

Extended multiple-choice question

Complete the following paragraph using the items listed below. Not all of the items will be consistent with the paragraph and not all items can be used. Items can be used only once.

_____ proposed the _____ of word recognition which was based on connectionist principles. Hence they theorised that there are three separate but interactive levels of recognition units. The lowest level of recognition occurs in the _____ where vertical, horizontal and circular aspects are identified. The middle level of recognition occurs in the _____ in which specific items are identified. The final level of recognition occurs in the word units in which the entire word is identified. Consistent with connectionism, discrimination of correct and competing units is achieved using _____ signals. For example, if vertical lines were detected at stage one the units corresponding to horizontal lines would be inhibited. Consequently, units corresponding to letters with horizontal lines would also be inhibited while the units corresponding to letters with vertical lines would be activated. Consequently, the model incorporates both bottom-up and top-down processing.

Optional items

A. Coltheart et al. (2001)

B. excitatory and inhibitory

C. feature units

D. interactive activation model

E. letter units

F. McClelland and Rumelhart (1981)

G. neuroscience

H. phonological

I. semantic

J. sentence reading

Essay questions for Chapter 8

Once you have completed the MCQs you are ready to tackle the example essay questions below. You might like to select three or four topics and make notes on them. One way of doing this is to create a concept map. The first question has been done for you and you can see how the knowledge required links to some of the MCQs in this chapter.

1. Critically discuss the extent to which language and communication are unique to humans.

2. Compare and contrast a minimum of two theories concerning language acquisition.

3. To what extent are the stages of language development universal?

4. Compare and contrast traditional theoretical, symbolic and connectionist models of language acquisition, comprehension and production.

5. Critically evaluate the theory of linguistic relativity with reference to both alternative theories and research.

6. Critically discuss evidence supporting the single-system and dual-system hypotheses concerning bilingualism, drawing conclusions concerning which is more plausible.

7. Compare and contrast the advantages and disadvantages of studying language in experimental and social contexts.

8. Critically evaluate the strengths and limitations of conducting research investigating cultural and gender differences in language.

Chapter 8 essay question 1: concept map

Critically discuss the extent to which language and communication are unique to humans.

The following concept map presents an example of how your responses to this question could be structured in a meaningful and comprehensive way. There are also links to specific questions in this chapter to guide your revision process. Human, animal and computation aspects of language are compared and contrasted.

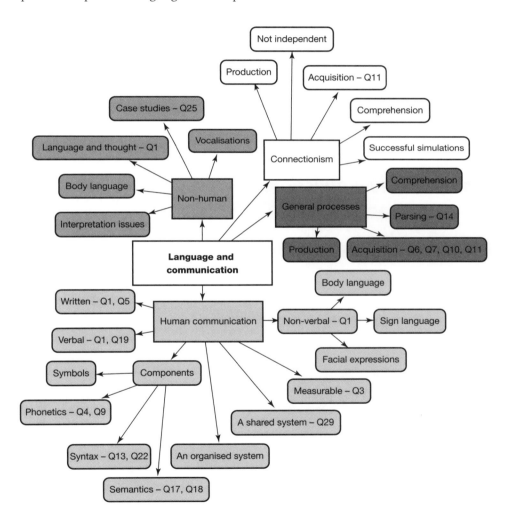

Chapter 9
Problem-solving, thinking and reasoning

This chapter provides questions relating to problem-solving, thinking and reasoning. It includes topics such as schools of thought, the scope of the subject, key terms and concepts, methodological considerations and prominent milestones in research. It will test both your foundation and advanced knowledge of these topics. At the end of the chapter are several example essay questions and a sample concept map which may enable you to organise your thoughts during essay planning.

Select one answer for each question.

Foundation level questions

1. How many stages are there in the problem-solving cycle?

   A. 9.

   B. 7.

   C. 10.

   D. 6.

Your answer: ☐

2. The concept of productive thinking was proposed by which of the following?

   A. Gestaltists.

   B. Behaviourists.

   C. Functionalists.

   D. Connectionists.

Your answer: ☐

3. The inability to conceptualise novel functions for an object is known as which of the following?

   A. Disconfirmation.

   B. Assimilation.

   C. Analogical encoding.

   D. Functional fixedness.

   Your answer: ☐

4. Analysis, synthesis, divergent thinking and convergent thinking can all be used during which stage of the problem-solving cycle?

   A. Problem identification.

   B. Strategy formulation.

   C. Problem representation.

   D. Organisation of information.

   Your answer: ☐

5. The total number of possible actions that can be applied to a given problem are often referred to as which of the following?

   A. Problem evaluation.

   B. Ill-defined problems.

   C. Problem space.

   D. Well-defined problems.

   Your answer: ☐

6. What name is given to informal and intuitive problem-solving strategies?

   A. Algorithms.

   B. Heuristics.

   C. Isomorphic.

   D. Adaptive control of thought.

   Your answer: ☐

7. Which of the following is not a heuristic?

A. Hierarchical computational rule.

B. Means-end analysis.

C. Generate and test.

D. Working backward.

Your answer: ☐

8. Changing the content but retaining the formal structure of a problem would make it which of the following?

A. Computational.

B. Ill-defined.

C. Well-defined.

D. Isomorphic.

Your answer: ☐

9. The two-string problem is an example of which form of problem?

A. Isomorphic.

B. Ill-structured.

C. Generate and test.

D. Means-end analysis.

Your answer: ☐

10. Selective-combination insights refer to which strategy?

A. Combining information in a novel and productive manner.

B. Undertaking means-end analyses.

C. Visual imagery.

D. Method of loci.

Your answer: ☐

11. Which of the following do not hinder problem-solving?

    A. Entrenchment.

    B. Fixation.

    C. Insight.

    D. Mental sets.

Your answer: ☐

Advanced level questions

12. Negative transfer refers to which of the following?

    A. When solving a previous problem aids solving a later problem.

    B. When retroactive interference occurs.

    C. When solving a previous problem hinders solving a later problem.

    D. When means-end analysis is counterproductive.

Your answer: ☐

13. Putting a problem aside for a period of time without consciously considering the problem in the interval is an example of which problem-solving aid?

    A. Transference.

    B. Incubation.

    C. Analogy.

    D. Method of loci.

Your answer: ☐

14. Chase and Simon (1973) investigated the differences in problem-solving for which two groups?

    A. Men and women.

    B. Older and younger adults.

    C. Drivers and pedestrians.

    D. Expert and novice chess players.

Your answer: ☐

15. Which of the following is true of expert knowledge?

    A. Better organisation, elaboration and automatisation of information than novices.

    B. Identical problem-solving strategies to those used by novices.

    C. Experts display better organisation skills than those displayed by novices.

    D. Experts display less automatic processing and more elaboration than novices.

Your answer: ☐

16. Which of the following contains an item which is not a form of creative contribution?

    A. Replication, forward movement and integration.

    B. Redirection, redefinition and starting over.

    C. Advance forward movement and redirection from a point in the past.

    D. None of the above.

Your answer: ☐

17. What is the term assigned to Simon's (1957) argument that humans are rational but within specific limits?

    A. Unbounded ideology.

    B. Satisficing.

    C. Bounded rationality.

    D. Subjective utility.

Your answer: ☐

18. Making judgements based on how easily information is called to mind uses which of the following?

    A. Schemata.

    B. Availability heuristic.

    C. Elimination by aspects.

    D. Anchoring-and-adjustment.

Your answer: ☐

19. In the case of conditional reasoning, which of the following pairs of terms is of paramount importance?

A. Truth and external validity.

B. Falsity and reliability.

C. Induction and logical soundness.

D. Deductive validity and logical soundness.

Your answer: ☐

20. Denying the antecedent is an example of which of the following?

A. Modus ponens.

B. Valid inferences.

C. Deductive fallacies.

D. Modus tollens.

Your answer: ☐

21. What is the name given to deductive arguments which draw conclusions based on two premises?

A. Algorithms.

B. Heuristics.

C. Syllogisms.

D. Confirmations.

Your answer: ☐

22. Which of the terms below reflect Sloman's (1996) theory of reasoning?

A. An inductive system and a deductive system.

B. An associative system and a rule-based system.

C. Premise-phrasing and overextension.

D. A deductive system and premise phrasing.

Your answer: ☐

Extended multiple-choice question

Complete the following diagram representing the problem-solving cycle using the items listed below. Not all of the items will be consistent with the diagram and not all items can be used. Items can be used only once.

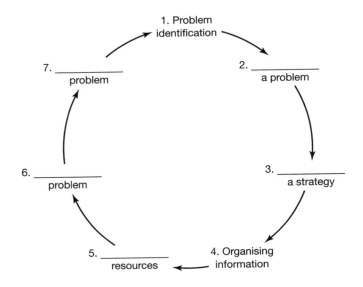

Optional items

A. Allocating

B. Constructing

C. Defining

D. Evaluating

E. Evoluting

F. Initiating

G. Monitoring

H. Reconstructing

I. Saving

J. Translating

Essay questions for Chapter 9

Once you have completed the MCQs you are ready to tackle the example essay questions below. You might like to select three or four topics and make notes on them. One way of doing this is to create a concept map. The first question has been done for you and you can see how the knowledge required links to some of the MCQs in this chapter.

1. Critically evaluate the validity of the Adaptive Control of Thought (ACT) model of problem-solving.

2. To what extent have Gestalt principles informed theories and research practices with regard to problem-solving?

3. Compare and contrast evidence concerning the strategies used during inductive and deductive reasoning.

4. Compare and contrast evidence and theories concerning the strategies used to solve well-defined and ill-structured problems.

5. To what extent can research investigating problem-solving be considered to be valid and reliable?

6. Critically evaluate a minimum of three aids which can be used during problem-solving.

7. To what extent have conventional experimental research and connectionist modelling contributed towards a comprehensive understanding of problem-solving and reasoning?

8. Compare and contrast research into heuristics and algorithms for problem-solving and reasoning.

Chapter 9 essay question 1: concept map

Critically evaluate the validity of the Adaptive Control of Thought (ACT) model of problem-solving.

The following concept map presents an example of how your responses to this question could be structured in a meaningful and comprehensive way. There are also links to specific questions in this chapter to guide your revision process. The ACT model of problem solving is evaluated with reference to the strengths, limitations, processes and alternative explanations.

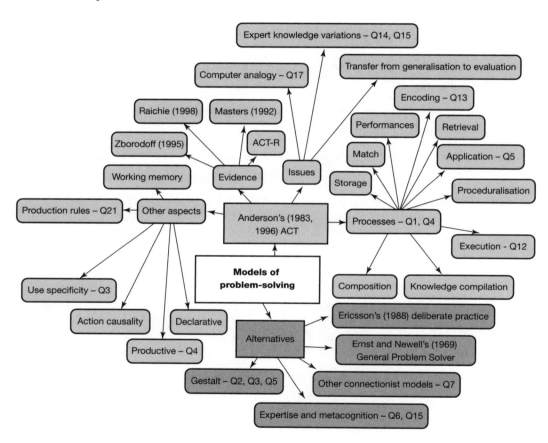

Chapter 10
Learning

This chapter provides questions relating to learning. It includes topics such as schools of thought, the scope of the subject, key terms and concepts, methodological considerations and prominent milestones in research. It will test both your foundation and advanced knowledge of these topics. At the end of the chapter are several example essay questions and a sample concept map which may enable you to organise your thoughts during essay planning.

Select one answer for each question.

Foundation level questions

1. Which of the following were Ebbinghaus's participants?

    A. Himself.

    B. School children.

    C. University students.

    D. Animals.

    Your answer: ☐

2. Which branch of psychology was primarily concerned with learning and observable behaviour but discounted the role of cognition?

    A. Introspection.

    B. Psychodynamic.

    C. Behaviourism.

    D. Neuroscience.

    Your answer: ☐

3. The tendency for learning to benefit from simply increasing the amount of time spent studying the material is known as which of the following?

A. Frequency hypothesis.

B. Residency hypothesis.

C. Heuristic hypothesis.

D. Total time hypothesis.

Your answer: ☐

4. Which of the following definitions is consistent with distributed practice?

A. Learning over several short sessions.

B. Learning over several long sessions.

C. Learning over several years.

D. Learning using two long sessions.

Your answer: ☐

5. The generation effect refers to which of the findings below?

A. Being provided with a reminder by an experimenter facilitates learning.

B. Learning can occur through random insight.

C. Producing a target word yourself facilitates learning.

D. Word association can produce generalisation of rules to other stimuli.

Your answer: ☐

6. Ericsson, Krampe and Tesch-Römer (1993) observed that which factor below contributed towards expertise in chess, typing and music?

A. Intelligence quotient.

B. Practice.

C. Genius as measured by Mensa.

D. Parental skill.

Your answer: ☐

7. Expanded retrieval refers to which experimental technique?

   A. Rapidly increasing the display time of stimuli to be learnt.

   B. Gradually allowing more explicit rehearsal time.

   C. Requiring more detailed responses.

   D. Gradually increasing the interval between learning and testing.

Your answer: ☐

8. What measure was found to enhance long-term memory by Marsh, Roediger, Bjork and Bjork (2007)?

   A. Verbal exams.

   B. Multiple choice.

   C. Group presentations.

   D. Essay questions.

Your answer: ☐

9. Pashler et al. (2007) provided what form of support during an exercise which aided learning?

   A. Direct feedback.

   B. Masked feedback.

   C. Training in the method of loci.

   D. Additional learning stages.

Your answer: ☐

10. Which of the following did Nilsson (1987) believe influenced learning but in actuality had no effect?

   A. Repetition.

   B. Feedback.

   C. Motivation.

   D. Vignettes.

Your answer: ☐

11. Complex information is unlikely to be learnt using which of the following?

   A. Elaborative rehearsal.

   B. Deep processing.

   C. Semantic processing.

   D. Saturation advertising.

Your answer: ☐

Advanced level questions

12. What percentage of participants demonstrated change blindness in Rosielle and Scaggs's (2008) study?

   A. 80.

   B. 40.

   C. 20.

   D. 50.

Your answer: ☐

13. Which of the following demonstrates an example of implicit learning?

   A. Learning course material for an exam.

   B. Learning to ride a bike.

   C. Learning a speech.

   D. Learning to recite multiplication tables.

Your answer: ☐

14. Breaking the association between a neutral stimulus and reward by presenting the neutral item independently produces which of the following according to behaviourism?

   A. Explicit knowledge.

   B. Behavioural alternatives.

   C. Latent inhibition.

   D. Rationality.

Your answer: ☐

15. What factor can provide a neutral item with positive value?

   A. Reconditioning.

   B. Repeated exposure.

   C. Extinction.

   D. Inhibition.

   Your answer: ☐

16. What was the pattern of results observed by Perfect and Askew (1994) with regard to the percentage of material learnt with and without instruction?

   A. 80% when not instructed to learn, 90% when instructed to learn.

   B. 50% when instructed to learn, 55% when not instructed to learn.

   C. 20% when not instructed to learn, 90% when instructed to learn.

   D. 60% when instructed to learn, 11% when not instructed to learn.

   Your answer: ☐

17. Which of the following techniques tests learning by presenting the first few letters of the target word?

   A. Stem completion.

   B. Fragment completion.

   C. Practice.

   D. Rehearsal.

   Your answer: ☐

18. Which of the follow conditions produced the best recall in Graf and Mandler's (1984) study?

   A. Completion based on semantic encoding.

   B. Cued retrieval based on semantic encoding.

   C. Cued retrieval based on physical encoding.

   D. Completion based on physical encoding.

   Your answer: ☐

19. Masters (1992) observed that providing a concurrent task during procedural learning produced which of the following?

A. Strategies remained explicit and subject to the effects of stress.

B. Strategies remained unconscious and less resistant to stress.

C. Strategies remained unconscious and more resistant to stress.

D. Strategies remained explicit and more resistant to stress.

Your answer: ☐

20. The state of consciousness where individuals are fully awake and alert was assigned which of the following terms by Damasio (1994)?

A. Core consciousness.

B. Base consciousness.

C. Advanced consciousness.

D. Primary consciousness.

Your answer: ☐

21. By which process would synaptic transmissions become more effective after a cell's recent activation according to the theory proposed by Bliss and Lomo (1973)?

A. Spreading activation.

B. Cell assembly.

C. Lesioning.

D. Long-term potentiation.

Your answer: ☐

22. SM and WC displayed double dissociation in which cortical regions respectively?

A. The amygdala and the hippocampus.

B. The amygdala and the hypothalamus.

C. The frontal lobe and the hippocampus.

D. The left temporal lobe and the right temporal lobe.

Your answer: ☐

Extended multiple-choice question

Complete the following paragraph using the items listed below. Not all of the items will be consistent with the paragraph and not all items can be used. Items can be used only once.

The study of learning processes and strategies can be applied across several areas including memory, language and problem-solving with regard to both intact and impaired cognition. For example, several _____ have been created to help individuals learn how to remember information. Indeed, the _____ requires that individuals employ imagery in an attempt to learn a series of objects. _____ also highlighted that simply providing the instruction to learn material significantly aided subsequent recall, demonstrating how motivation and instruction may be related to learning. However, with regard to neuropsychology and memory, individuals with _____ often find it difficult to learn new information regardless of learning aid. With regard to problem-solving, the study of expertise demonstrates that individuals varying in proficiency employ very different _____.

Optional items

A. anterograde amnesia

B. comprehension

C. imagery

D. learning aids

E. method of loci

F. motivation and instruction

G. retrograde amnesia

H. Maccoby (1990)

I. Perfect and Askew (1994)

J. strategies

Essay questions for Chapter 10

Once you have completed the MCQs you are ready to tackle the example essay questions below. You might like to select three or four topics and make notes on them. One way of doing this is to create a concept map. The first question has been done for you and you can see how the knowledge required links to some of the MCQs in this chapter.

1. Compare and contrast a minimum of two theoretical accounts of learning.

2. To what extent have experimental techniques been generalised to learning from alternative areas of study?

3. Evaluate the contributions made by behaviourism and cognitive science towards a coherent understanding of learning.

4. Critically discuss the strengths and limitations of studying learning in non-human animals.

5. Compare and contrast the insights into learning provided by case studies in neuropsychology and computer simulations.

6. To what extent are consciousness, motivation and instruction required for successful learning?

7. To what extent does the study of learning inform other areas of cognitive psychology?

8. Critically discuss the claim that behaviourism no longer contributes reliable insight regarding human learning.

Chapter 10 essay question 1: concept map

Compare and contrast a minimum of two theoretical accounts of learning.

The following concept map presents an example of how your responses to this question could be structured in a meaningful and comprehensive way. There are also links to specific questions in this chapter to guide your revision process. Three different models of learning (operant conditioning, classical conditioning and social learning) are compared and contrasted with reference to each aspect of these theories.

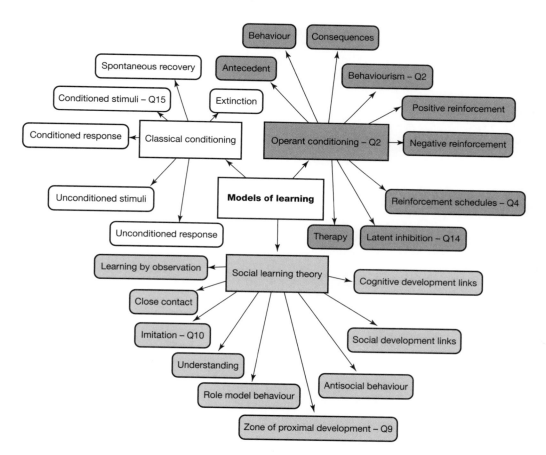

Writing an essay: a format for success

The following bullet points provide you with some general guidance for essay writing in cognitive psychology and are intended to assist you in formulating and arranging your arguments. However, remember that the structure may vary according to topic and the nature of the essay question. For further guidance concerning the style advocated by the American Psychological Association please consult the APA guidelines.

- All essays should begin with a brief introduction summarising the scope and direction of your response to the question and the conclusions which will be drawn. You should assume that the reader of your essay will have no previous knowledge of the subject and so write as clearly and explicitly as possible.

- It is recommended that you establish your stance early in the essay to provide a strong foundation for debate and consideration of evidence.

- The next section of your essay should briefly present the theories which will be critically evaluated throughout the essay. All technical terms should be clearly defined to demonstrate knowledge and make the essay accessible to the reader. The original sources for the theories and any relevant adaptations should be cited fully in the APA format.

- All of the relevant aspects of the theories should be discussed, evaluated and, ideally, compared. For example, does one of the theories present a more comprehensive account than the alternative perspectives or do the theories review the same phenomenon at complementary but alternative levels of analysis? The student should also make explicit references to how an analysis of each theory would facilitate a response to the question.

- You must also be careful to establish a balance between descriptive and critical writing. For example, essays which compare and contrast perspectives and evidence will achieve better results than those which only reiterate information with no analysis.

- Research evidence supporting and refuting each theory should be presented and critically reviewed. This evidence should be synthesised rather than simply restated. For example, does the majority of evidence support one theory or are there remaining flaws with the account? All sources must be cited fully and should be drawn from appropriate material.

- Always link each paragraph back to the essay question to explain how the text has answered the question and to maintain a clear progression in your argument.

- Base your conclusion on the weight of the evidence supporting each argument. The conclusion should be written clearly with direct links back to the essay question. While the consideration of the evidence should be balanced, this does not prevent you from adopting a perspective.

- All sources used throughout the essay should be cited in APA format in a reference list if the essay is submitted as an assignment. If the essay is submitted in examination conditions, the guidelines for your particular institution should be consulted.

Scoring methods in MCQs

Introduction

All assessments need to be reviewed and marked. At your university you will come across a number of formal (often called summative) and informal (aka formative) assessments. These can take the form of practical reports, essays, short-answer questions and (of course) examinations. There are, of course, a number of forms of examinations – short answers, written essays and multiple-choice questions (or MCQs).

MCQs are considered objective assessments, that is answers are unambiguously correct or incorrect and therefore provide for high marker reliability – so that's one positive mark for MCQs. On the other hand, there is often a concern (for the examination setter) that guessing by the candidate can have an inflationary influence on the marks. By chance, if you have four choices then you should score 25% just by guessing. This is obviously not a situation to be encouraged, and because of this your psychology course team may have introduced various attempts to make sure that this does not happen. It is worth exploring some of these methods and the implications these will have for the approach you take to your assessment and, ultimately, how they can impact on your examination performance.

Scoring of MCQ examinations can take several forms. At its most simple, a raw score is calculated based on the total number of correct responses (usually 1 mark per correct answer). Under this approach, any omissions or incorrect responses earn you no marks but neither do they attract a penalty. If you get the question right, you get a mark; if you do not then you get no mark.

As mentioned, alternative and more complex approaches to marking have been developed because of concerns that results can be inflated if correct responses are the result of successful guessing. The most common approaches to discouraging random guessing include the reward of partial knowledge and negative marking. This can impact on your behaviour and your learning. Of course, whatever the examination and whatever the marking scheme, you need to know your stuff!

Rewarding partial knowledge

Scoring procedures developed to reward partial knowledge are based on the assumption that though you and your student colleagues may be unable to identify a single correct response you can confidently identify some options as being incorrect and that partial knowledge should therefore be rewarded. Versions of this approach generally allow you to choose:

- more than one possibly correct response and to be awarded a partial mark provided one of your responses is the correct answer;
- a 'not sure' option for which you are awarded a proportion of a mark (usually either 0.2 or 0.25).

Negative marking

Negative marking is when your performance is based on the total number of correct responses which is then reduced in some way to correct for any potential guessing. The simplest application of negative marking is where equal numbers of marks are added or subtracted for right and wrong answers and omitted answers or the selection of a 'No answer' option that has no impact on marks. So, you get +1 mark when you get the question right, –1 mark when you get it wrong and 0 if you do not attempt it. However, there are other approaches which are slightly more punitive. In these approaches, if you get the question correct you get +1, if you get the question wrong then this is awarded a –1 (or even –2) and if there is no attempt then this is awarded a –1 as well as, it is suggested, you do not know the answer.

How does this impact on you?

The impact of these scoring mechanisms can be significant. By way of example, use the following table to demonstrate your performance in each of the chapters in this text. For each of the chapters work out the number of correct responses (and code this as NC), the number of incorrect answers (coded as NI) and the number of questions that you did not provide a response to (NR). You can then use the formulae in the table to work out how you would have performed under each of the different marking schemes. For example, for the punitive negative marking scheme you score 18 correct (NC=18), 2 incorrect (NI=2) and omitted 5 questions (NR=5). On the basis of the formula in the table, NC-(NI*2)-NR, you would have scored 9 (i.e. 18-(2*2)-5). So even though you managed to get 18 out of 25 this would have been reduced to only 9 because of the punitive marking.

Chapter	Number correct	Number incorrect	No response	Marking scheme: raw score	Marking scheme: partial knowledge	Marking scheme: negative marking	Marking scheme: punitive negative marking
	NC	NI	NR	= NC	= NC − (NI * 0.2)	= NC − NI	= NC − (NI * 2) − NR
1							
2							
3							
4							
5							
6							
7							
8							
9							
10							
TOTAL							

Explore the scores above – which chapter did you excel at and for which chapter do you need to do some work? Use the above table to see your areas of strength and areas of weakness – and consequently where you need to spend more time revising and reviewing the material.

MCQ answers

Chapter 1: Introduction to cognitive psychology – MCQ answers

Level	Question number	Correct response	Self-monitoring
Foundation	1	D	
Foundation	2	B	
Foundation	3	C	
Foundation	4	A	
Foundation	5	D	
Foundation	6	C	
Foundation	7	A	
Foundation	8	B	
Foundation	9	A	
Foundation	10	D	
Foundation	11	C	
Advanced	12	A	
Advanced	13	B	
Advanced	14	B	
Advanced	15	C	
Advanced	16	D	
Advanced	17	A	
Advanced	18	C	
Advanced	19	D	
Advanced	20	B	
Advanced	21	A	
Advanced	22	A	
Advanced	23	D	
Advanced	24	C	
		Total number of points:	Foundation: Advanced:

EMCQ for Chapter 1

The paragraph should read as follows. A maximum of 5 points can be allocated.

Laboratory-based experiments in cognitive psychology present the opportunity to manipulate a series of <u>independent variables</u> and identify how they impact upon the <u>dependent variables</u> within a controlled environment. These experiments possess significant validity and <u>reliability</u> when performed correctly. However, multiple-methods often expand the understanding of phenomena. For example, <u>neuroimaging</u> can be combined with traditional experimentation to assess the physiological responses and corresponding cortical activity. <u>Case studies</u> in neuropsychology can be combined with traditional experimentation to assess how normal functions may be impaired following brain damage or infection. With regard to connectionism, this technique can be utilised to assess the micro-processes of cognition using computer simulations.

Chapter 2: Perception – MCQ answers

Level	Question number	Correct response	Self-monitoring
Foundation	1	B	
Foundation	2	A	
Foundation	3	D	
Foundation	4	A	
Foundation	5	C	
Foundation	6	B	
Foundation	7	B	
Foundation	8	C	
Foundation	9	A	
Foundation	10	D	
Foundation	11	C	
Foundation	12	A	
Foundation	13	B	
Advanced	14	A	
Advanced	15	C	
Advanced	16	D	
Advanced	17	B	
Advanced	18	B	
Advanced	19	C	
Advanced	20	A	
Advanced	21	A	
Advanced	22	D	
Advanced	23	B	
Advanced	24	C	
Advanced	25	A	
Advanced	26	D	
		Total number of points:	Foundation: Advanced:

EMCQ for Chapter 2

The paragraph should read as follows. A maximum of 5 points can be allocated.

The Berlin School, from which the <u>Gestalt approach</u> emerged, argued that the brain functions in a holistic manner with a tendency to impose organisation on seemingly random configurations. Consequently, they argued that the entirety of the perceived image takes precedence over the individual components. This is in direct comparison to previous perspectives which drew on <u>structuralism</u> such as that advocated by Wundt. Gestalt theorists proposed several principles which can be directly applied to perception. For example, <u>psychophysical isomorphism</u> states that there is direct correspondence between conscious experience and the activity observed in the brain. Significantly, the principle of <u>contiguity</u> also states that items which are organised in close proximity tend to be perceived as belonging together. Such theories are often demonstrated using <u>optical illusions</u>.

Chapter 3: Attention – MCQ answers

Level	Question number	Correct response	Self-monitoring
Foundation	1	A	
Foundation	2	B	
Foundation	3	C	
Foundation	4	A	
Foundation	5	D	
Foundation	6	C	
Foundation	7	A	
Foundation	8	B	
Foundation	9	D	
Foundation	10	C	
Foundation	11	C	
Advanced	12	A	
Advanced	13	B	
Advanced	14	A	
Advanced	15	D	
Advanced	16	C	
Advanced	17	A	
Advanced	18	C	
Advanced	19	B	
Advanced	20	B	
Advanced	21	D	
Advanced	22	A	
Advanced	23	C	
		Total number of points:	Foundation: Advanced:

EMCQ for Chapter 3

The items should read as follows. A maximum of 5 points can be allocated.

- Numerous sources of information are present in the environment.
- Information is processed through the <u>sensory</u> register.
- The <u>selective</u> filter focuses on one channel of information.
- <u>Perceptual</u> processes are initiated to process basic features about the stimuli.
- Information is transmitted and stored briefly in <u>short-term</u> memory.
- A <u>response</u> is made dependent upon the task and attentional processes.

Chapter 4: Models of memory – MCQ answers

Level	Question number	Correct response	Self-monitoring
Foundation	1	B	
Foundation	2	A	
Foundation	3	C	
Foundation	4	C	
Foundation	5	D	
Foundation	6	A	
Foundation	7	C	
Foundation	8	B	
Foundation	9	A	
Foundation	10	D	
Advanced	11	A	
Advanced	12	B	
Advanced	13	C	
Advanced	14	D	
Advanced	15	B	
Advanced	16	A	
Advanced	17	B	
Advanced	18	D	
Advanced	19	C	
Advanced	20	A	
		Total number of points:	Foundation: Advanced:

EMCQ for Chapter 4

The model should look as follows. A maximum of 5 points can be allocated.

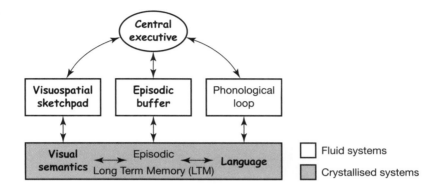

Chapter 5: Applied aspects of memory – MCQ answers

Level	Question number	Correct response	Self-monitoring
Foundation	1	C	
Foundation	2	B	
Foundation	3	B	
Foundation	4	D	
Foundation	5	A	
Foundation	6	C	
Foundation	7	B	
Foundation	8	A	
Foundation	9	C	
Foundation	10	D	
Foundation	11	B	
Advanced	12	A	
Advanced	13	A	
Advanced	14	C	
Advanced	15	B	
Advanced	16	D	
Advanced	17	C	
Advanced	18	B	
Advanced	19	A	
Advanced	20	C	
Advanced	21	A	
		Total number of points:	Foundation: Advanced:

EMCQ for Chapter 5

The paragraph should read as follows. A maximum of 6 points can be allocated.

<u>Bartlett (1932)</u> employed the method of <u>serial reproduction</u> and demonstrated the reconstructive nature of memory. This technique includes copying a drawing from memory or recounting a story in the same format. Participants often reconstruct elements of the story or drawing to make it consistent with their own <u>cultural</u> and personal expectations irrespective of the actual items encountered during the task. Bartlett (1932) theorised that the memory distortions observed using this task arise due to the influence of schemata. However, schema theory originated in the work by <u>Piaget (1926)</u>. <u>Loftus and Palmer (1974)</u> demonstrated how reconstructive memory and leading questions can also influence the accuracy of eyewitness testimony. A second example of how schemas may influence recall is demonstrated by <u>confabulation</u>. This refers to the phenomenon in which participants combine elements of a story or fill in the gaps in their memory with plausible alternatives in states of high motivation and emotion.

Chapter 6: Cognition and emotion – MCQ answers

Level	Question number	Correct response	Self-monitoring
Foundation	1	A	
Foundation	2	C	
Foundation	3	B	
Foundation	4	A	
Foundation	5	D	
Foundation	6	B	
Foundation	7	C	
Foundation	8	B	
Foundation	9	D	
Foundation	10	A	
Foundation	11	C	
Advanced	12	A	
Advanced	13	D	
Advanced	14	C	
Advanced	15	B	
Advanced	16	D	
Advanced	17	A	
Advanced	18	B	
Advanced	19	C	
Advanced	20	B	
Advanced	21	D	
Advanced	22	A	
		Total number of points:	Foundation: Advanced:

EMCQ for Chapter 6

The paragraph should read as follows. A maximum of 5 points can be allocated.

The study of emotion and cognition demonstrates a significant example of how numerous schools of thought have attempted to describe phenomena. For example, from a <u>cognitive</u> perspective, <u>Simon (1967)</u> argued that emotions set the <u>priorities</u> of any intelligent being and are therefore extrinsically linked to cognition. Indeed, emotional responses can determine, or be in response to, cognitive <u>appraisal,</u> thought, goals and actions. However, <u>evolutionary</u> theories also state that some behaviours and responses may be determined by reflexes which benefit the organism's chances of survival. For example, in the case of threatening stimuli, the startle response may arise rapidly and without conscious appraisal. Furthermore, the behaviourist school of thought would suggest that the associations formed during this process could account for anxiety and phobias.

Chapter 7: Cognitive neuropsychology – MCQ answers

Level	Question number	Correct response	Self-monitoring
Foundation	1	A	
Foundation	2	C	
Foundation	3	D	
Foundation	4	C	
Foundation	5	D	
Foundation	6	A	
Foundation	7	B	
Foundation	8	D	
Foundation	9	A	
Foundation	10	D	
Foundation	11	C	
Foundation	12	B	
Foundation	13	A	
Advanced	14	D	
Advanced	15	B	
Advanced	16	C	
Advanced	17	A	
Advanced	18	D	
Advanced	19	B	
Advanced	20	D	
Advanced	21	C	
Advanced	22	A	
Advanced	23	B	
Advanced	24	D	
Advanced	25	C	
Advanced	26	A	
		Total number of points:	Foundation: Advanced:

EMCQ for Chapter 7

The paragraph should read as follows. A maximum of 5 points can be allocated.

Cognitive neuropsychology investigates normal and impaired cognitive functioning using a wide variety of experimental techniques. These can include detailed <u>case studies</u> of neurologically impaired patients and <u>cohort studies</u> in which the performance of matched unimpaired and impaired participants are compared. Hence, traditional experimental techniques, advanced technology and observation are often combined. For example, <u>neuroimaging</u> techniques can be used to identify the cerebral structures and activity associated with specific tasks and forms of cognition. <u>Functional magnetic resonance imaging</u> can be used to identify the change in blood flow and oxygenation associated with neural activity. In contrast <u>positron emission tomography</u> can be used to produce a three-dimensional image reflecting cerebral structures and activity using a positron-emitting radionuclide. A range of traditional experimental techniques have also been developed, including measures of memory and perceptual and linguistic processing.

Chapter 8: Language – MCQ answers

Level	Question number	Correct response	Self-monitoring
Foundation	1	D	
Foundation	2	B	
Foundation	3	A	
Foundation	4	A	
Foundation	5	C	
Foundation	6	D	
Foundation	7	D	
Foundation	8	B	
Foundation	9	C	
Foundation	10	A	
Foundation	11	C	
Foundation	12	B	
Foundation	13	D	
Foundation	14	B	
Foundation	15	C	
Advanced	16	A	
Advanced	17	D	
Advanced	18	B	
Advanced	19	C	
Advanced	20	B	
Advanced	21	A	
Advanced	22	D	
Advanced	23	C	
Advanced	24	A	
Advanced	25	B	
Advanced	26	D	
Advanced	27	B	
Advanced	28	C	
Advanced	29	A	
Advanced	30	C	
		Total number of points:	Foundation: Advanced:

EMCQ for Chapter 8

The paragraph should read as follows. A maximum of 5 points can be allocated.

<u>McClelland and Rumelhart (1981)</u> proposed the <u>interactive activation model</u> of word recognition which was based on connectionist principles. Hence, they theorised that there are three separate but interactive levels of recognition units. The lowest level of recognition occurs in the <u>feature units</u> where vertical, horizontal and circular aspects are identified. The middle level of recognition occurs in the <u>letter units</u> in which specific items are identified. The final level of recognition occurs in the word units in which the entire word is identified. Consistent with connectionism, discrimination of correct and competing units is achieved using <u>excitatory and inhibitory</u> signals. For example, if vertical lines were detected at stage one the units corresponding to horizontal lines would be inhibited. Consequently, units corresponding to letters with horizontal lines would also be inhibited while the units corresponding to letters with vertical lines would be activated. Consequently, the model incorporates both bottom-up and top-down processing.

Chapter 9: Problem-solving, thinking and reasoning – MCQ answers

Level	Question number	Correct response	Self-monitoring
Foundation	1	B	
Foundation	2	A	
Foundation	3	D	
Foundation	4	B	
Foundation	5	C	
Foundation	6	B	
Foundation	7	A	
Foundation	8	D	
Foundation	9	B	
Foundation	10	A	
Foundation	11	C	
Advanced	12	C	
Advanced	13	B	
Advanced	14	D	
Advanced	15	A	
Advanced	16	D	
Advanced	17	C	
Advanced	18	B	
Advanced	19	D	
Advanced	20	A	
Advanced	21	C	
Advanced	22	B	
		Total number of points:	Foundation: Advanced:

EMCQ for Chapter 9

The correct problem solving cycle is provided below. A maximum of 5 points can be allocated.

1. Problem identification

2. **Defining** a problem

3. **Constructing** a strategy

4. Organising information

5. **Allocating** resources

6. **Monitoring** problem

7. **Evaluating** problem

Chapter 10: Learning – MCQ answers

Level	Question number	Correct response	Self-monitoring
Foundation	1	A	
Foundation	2	C	
Foundation	3	D	
Foundation	4	A	
Foundation	5	C	
Foundation	6	B	
Foundation	7	D	
Foundation	8	B	
Foundation	9	A	
Foundation	10	C	
Foundation	11	D	
Advanced	12	A	
Advanced	13	B	
Advanced	14	C	
Advanced	15	B	
Advanced	16	D	
Advanced	17	A	
Advanced	18	B	
Advanced	19	C	
Advanced	20	A	
Advanced	21	D	
Advanced	22	A	
		Total number of points:	Foundation: Advanced:

EMCQ for Chapter 10

The paragraph should read as follows. A maximum of 5 points can be allocated.

The study of learning processes and strategies can be applied across several areas including memory, language and problem-solving with regard to both intact and impaired cognition. For example, several <u>learning aids</u> have been created to help individuals learn how to remember information. Indeed, the <u>method of loci</u> requires that individuals employ imagery in an attempt to learn a series of objects. <u>Perfect and Askew (1994)</u> also highlighted that simply providing the instruction to learn material significantly aided subsequent recall, demonstrating how motivation and instruction may be related to learning. However, in regard to neuropsychology and memory, individuals with <u>anterograde amnesia</u> often find it difficult to learn new information regardless of learning aid. In regard to problem-solving, the study of expertise demonstrates that individuals varying in proficiency employ very different <u>strategies</u>.